THE AIRPORT ECONOMIST

The airport economist has a website
www.theairporteconomist.com

THE AIRPORT ECONOMIST

Tim Harcourt

ALLEN&UNWIN

First published in 2008

Copyright © Tim Harcourt 2008

Allen & Unwin
83 Alexander Street
Crows Nest NSW 2065
Australia
Phone: (61 2) 8425 0100
Fax: (61 2) 9906 2218
Email: info@allenandunwin.com
Web: www.allenandunwin.com

National Library of Australia
Cataloguing-in-Publication entry:

  Harcourt, Tim.
  The airport economist / Tim Harcourt.

  Crows Nest, N.S.W. : Allen & Unwin, 2008.

  9781741755121 (pbk.)

  Exports—Economic aspects—Australia.
  Foreign trade promotion—Australia

Set in New Baskerville 10/12 pt by Midland Typesetters, Australia
Printed and bound in Australia by McPherson's Printing Group
10 9 8 7 6 5 4 3 2 1

CONTENTS

INTRODUCTION

ONCE UPON A time, in the 1970s, when stagflation (double-digit inflation and unemployment) ravaged western economies, economists were dispatched to lands near and far to offer 'advice' (some for free, some paid for). A famous example was in 1974 when the father of the Chicago School of economics, the late Milton Friedman, visited Australia to offer his advice to policymakers down under. Friedman, well known for his economic advice to the Pinochet regime in Chile, suggested the usual medicine to Australian policy-makers: Fight inflation first by using monetary policy, balance the budget, deregulate the financial markets, and reduce the size of government. However, Friedman gave this advice at a hastily arranged press conference at the airport *on arrival* in Australia, before he had got the chance to examine conditions in Australia and meet with Australian officials. As a result, local opponents of his policies coined the term 'airport economist' for Friedman.

Since then, a number of airport economists have been identified, some also bestowing wisdom upon a country without actually leaving the airport arrivals lounge. Take Jeffrey Sachs, who flew around the world giving advice to the transition economies after the fall of communism and also in Latin America before becoming a strong anti-poverty campaigner. During the Asian financial crisis of 1997–99, the likes of Indonesia had many visits from airport economists, particularly those with the International Monetary Fund (IMF) and the World Bank. Unfortunately for the IMF (and even more so for the countries involved) identical policy advice was offered to several countries on one whirlwind trip (and, embarrassingly, someone forgot to proofread an otherwise standard document so that, for example, the word 'Malaysia' wasn't replaced by the word 'Indonesia' when required). This particular incident revived the original basis of the 'airport economist' concept, that there is a one-size-fits-all approach to policy, and that visits to actual countries are more for show than investigation.

However, all that is really just a quick history lesson on the term and not in fact why I called this book *The Airport Economist*. I have always wanted to write an economics book and have a particular interest in how economic integration on a global scale affects local communities. On the other hand, I have always wanted to write what is sometimes dubbed an 'airport book', that is, one that is accessible and read by lots of people! Like many travellers, I do much of my reading on planes and find airport bookstores fantastic value. So, like a true 'two-handed' economist wanting to write both an economics and an airport book, I decided *The Airport Economist* had to be the answer.

So why did the airport economist choose the destinations he travelled to? It was a matter of covering the world in a vaguely comprehensive fashion and also going to places where Australia has a reasonable (if in some cases developing) economic presence. It was also important to get the balance right between Asia, Europe and the Americas whilst finding some room for emerging markets in the Middle East and Africa.

But you can't go everywhere (man). Criticised by some for travelling too much as prime minister of Australia, when one of Gough Whitlam's staffers reported that the United

Nations had created three brand new countries, Gough allegedly replied (with a touch of sarcasm): 'The UN is creating countries faster than I can f****** well visit them!' Well, the UN is creating countries faster than the airport economist can visit them but you have to make a start somewhere. In any case, as my publisher said, we had to leave some countries for the sequel.

The airport economist's journey was greatly assisted by access to the Australian Trade Commission's global network. The Australian Trade Commission—better known within Australia as Austrade—is the federal government agency that helps Australian companies crack the global economy. Traditionally, Austrade has helped Australian companies to export, but with new forms of globalisation sweeping international business Austrade has also supported Australian companies to set up joint ventures, strategic alliances, licensing and franchising arrangements, international aid procurement and foreign direct investment. The Austrade global network covers 62 countries with nearly 120 locations. If the domestic network is added, Austrade has coverage from Adelaide to Zagreb.

Naturally, because of the nationality of the airport economist and his association with Austrade, this book takes on an Australian flavour. However, whilst *The Airport Economist* mainly focuses on opportunities for Australians in the world and looks principally at trade and commercial questions, I hope that both non-Australians and non-economists (who may not get as excited as I do about the wonderful world of trade and economics) will still enjoy the ride. In particular, I hope that students—both Australian and international— might find trade and economics as interesting as I do and even consider a career with an international focus. In addition, I hope that some small businesspeople and budding entrepreneurs out there, who hadn't thought a lot about the opportunities of the global economy before, decide to stick their own toe in the water beyond our shores.

ASIA

1 EVERYBODY LOVES RAYMOND

Why is Singapore more famous for its engineers than for its ballet dancers? What is the new Singaporean obsession with 'creativity'? The airport economist investigates.

THERE'S NO DOUBT about it, Singapore works. If you like order, cleanliness, intelligence and efficiency then you'll like Singapore. Singapore is not very big—just a city on an island, really—but as a regional economic player in Southeast Asia and beyond it has done very well on all counts. The city-state has transformed itself from a relatively poor nation in the 1960s to an affluent, service-based economy with living standards at OECD levels—well ahead of most of its Southeast Asian neighbours. Singapore has almost become a 'Switzerland of Asia', with its strengths in international banking and finance.

So what is the reason for Singapore's success? One is education. Singaporeans are just so damn smart. In fact, the airport economist himself is a beneficiary of the Singapore brain-fest. When I was studying economics at the University of Adelaide, most of the students in the year ahead of me were from Singapore or Malaysia. They were literally my neighbours, too, as we shared a dorm corridor in a residential college. All this happened by chance as this group of students—some of Singapore's best and brightest—were meant to go to Oxford to study nuclear physics and become rocket scientists, but a glitch in Singapore's otherwise near perfect education allocation-cum-manpower planning system meant they ended up in Adelaide studying economics with me.

This mix-up had two consequences, the first immediate, the second more long-term in nature.

The first consequence was that I was suddenly surrounded by all this brainpower, particularly in quantitative, technical subjects like mathematics, statistics and econometrics. Accordingly, my grades in these difficult subjects were greatly enhanced thanks to my Singaporean classmates/corridor neighbours. Economists often talk about 'externalities' or 'spillovers', which refers to a private action having social consequences which are not factored in to the original decision. Usually spillovers are negative, such as when a private factory pollutes a river (which causes social costs not accounted for in the initial commercial decision). However, there can be positive externalities or spillovers too. In this case, the Singaporeans' talents at mathematical economics 'spilled over' into my orbit as they helped me to understand the difficult techniques required to excel at the coursework.

Fortunately, there were 'gains from trade' to be had. Economists also often talk about 'comparative advantage'. The theory goes that if you are relatively good at something you should trade with the person who is relatively good at something else. It works for nations as well as people. So when it came to writing economic essays—particularly of thesis length—I was able to help my classmates and pay them back for the help they gave me with quantitative methods.

The second consequence came to light many years after we all graduated. Over time, all these talented Singaporeans have ended up back home running the place. Adelaide has made its mark on Singaporean public life—at the highest levels.

Probably the most famous example from my university days is Raymond Lim, a new young gun in the Singaporean government. Lim has held a number of high-level portfolios including Minister for Transport, Minister for Trade and Industry, and Minister for Foreign Affairs. Like his namesake from the Grammy-winning US television series *Everybody Loves Raymond*, Lim is clearly a man to watch in business and political circles in the city-state. One of the 'magnificent seven' (a group of seven emerging politicians hand-picked by then Prime Minister Goh Chok Tong), Lim is responsible for ensuring that Singapore remains competitive and innovative in the post-industrial age. When the airport economist met Lim at his office in Singapore, he was upbeat about his country's prospects. 'We are keen to nurture our creative industries and encourage innovation in the new Singapore,' he explained. 'Singapore is a high-income, mature economy with many knowledge-based industries. In this environment, our best chance is to encourage building our own human capital, support local entrepreneurship and to encourage other countries' businesses to base themselves here in Singapore.'

One example of the 'incubator' approach is Singapore's Torch Centre, a base for 25,000 small- and medium-sized enterprises (SMEs) from China. The Torch Centre provides a launch pad for SME internationalisation to the rest of Southeast Asia and beyond. Lim says foreign ownership is not an issue in an *entrepot* economy like Singapore: 'We don't mind if they're not Singapore-owned, we just want them to be Singapore-based.' It is hoped that, once again, Singapore can use its comparative advantage to great effect: without vast land, natural resources or a large population, the city-state has had to use its knowledge and capacity to be an international business hub to succeed. I guess it has got to be said that Singapore has a pretty good track record on this score, so the incubator approach should help the city-state to continue its winning streak well into the future.

So that's the good news. There's no doubt that Singapore is efficient and clean and its citizens are, on average, highly intelligent and well-educated, but there is something missing. What happens when a nation can produce lots of engineers but very few ballet dancers, or plenty of world-class superannuation fund managers but few artists or novelists? Well, to be frank, it becomes just a little bit dull. In short, Singapore needs a bit of livening up on the creative front, some left-brain stuff to go with its already impressive, almost exploding, right-brain achievements.

That's what Raymond Lim told me that he and his generation of hot-shot legislators wanted to change about their island home. Lim wants Singaporeans to unleash their creativity on the world (or at least on each other in the first instance).

They certainly have been trying. Singapore's 'renaissance' in arts and culture is symbolised by the new durian-shaped concert hall seen as you drive into town from Changi Airport. To the uninitiated, the durian (Singapore's national fruit) has a most unusual smell but a fabulous taste. It also has an important symbolic place in the Singaporean heart, so while Sydney has its eggshell-shaped Opera House, Singapore has its durian.

In multimedia, too, Singapore's creative industries have made some progress. For example, Lim is very proud of the fact that in a global competition to develop documentaries for the National Geographic channel in Asia, six out of the ten winners were Singapore-based.

However, despite these promising signs, there's something funny going on. The creativity campaign, like all things Singaporean, seems very systematic and planned. For instance, a number of government buildings display 'Be Creative' banners in their foyers and there's even talk of having all Singaporeans attend mandatory creativity classes on Saturday morning, from 10am to 11.30am sharp. Sure, there's plenty of evidence that creativity can have economic benefits as economist Richard Florida showed in his seminal book, *The Rise of the Creative Class. And how it's transforming work, leisure and everyday life* about US cities with a high proportion of creative industry workers or 'creative classes' (as well as ethnically diverse and gay populations). But can creativity be, well, 'created' by a government regulation? It remains to be seen.

In any case, whether legislated or not, Singapore's creativity drive is creating some unique opportunities for Australia which, as a nation of sports junkies, actually does very well on the creative exports side. For instance, the Sydney-based Bell Shakespeare Company has brought drama education to Singapore. Company founder and national treasure John Bell sees Singapore and Shanghai as the focal points for Bell Shakespeare's mission to bring Shakespearean method to Asian students with an Australian style. 'Drama is about performance, but also training and education. We have had great success in helping budding Singaporean actors learn about theatre. It has been a great education for us as well,' Bell explains. As a result of Bell Shakespeare's foray into the drama market, Singapore may well become a land fit for thespians.

Creativity is the latest injection into Australia's economic relationship with Singapore, which had mainly been based on services, including in professional areas such as architecture, financial services and education.

Architectural design is an important area for Australian services exporters in Asia, and Singapore has been a great launching pad. In fact, despite all the so-called arts versus sports debates that we have in Australia, there are examples where sport has actually *helped* creative exports—especially in the case of design. Take the example of the Sydney-based architectural firm Woodhead. In 2000 the firm's principals were seated next to several Singapore Airlines executives at the Sydney Olympics as part of the Business Club Australia (BCA) programme (a sort of matchmaking club for exporters set around major sporting events). As a result of this meeting, Woodhead won two major contracts. The first was to design the interiors at Changi Airport's Terminal 3, which houses Singapore Airlines—a project estimated to have been worth around S$1.4 billion (A$1.35 billion). The second project was the design of the interiors at Singapore's National Library (worth around S$230 million or A$222 million). This is big bickies for an architectural firm.

Even though Woodhead has been in business since 1927, it has only just been able to enter global markets. According to Woodhead's principal, Robert Hopton, whom the airport economist actually met in a taxi queue *at the airport*, the Singapore deals have enabled the firm—now known as Woodhead International—to break into Thailand, Malaysia, India, Nepal and, of course, China. One reason for its success has been its professional openness to sharing knowledge. As Robert Hopton explains: 'Success begets success. Our willingness to partner with others and share information has been one of our greatest assets. It is an excellent way of growing new opportunities and building your capacity to enter new markets.' Instead of keeping all the knowledge close to its chest, the firm practised the principle of 'share and share alike' with its business partners and received a positive response and a return flow of information.

Woodhead International is just the sort of Australian professional services company that has benefited from the Singapore–Australia Free Trade Agreement (SAFTA), the first bilateral trade agreement for Australia since the conclusion of the Australia–New Zealand Closer Economic Relations (CER) agreement over two decades ago. Before SAFTA, foreign architects had to run their plans through the offices of the Singapore government architect, which meant delays and frustratingly slow business as a result. Under SAFTA, an Aussie architect is treated like a local, so it is more of a level playing field. According to Hopton, 'Getting a foothold in Singapore really helped us take off in Asia. And it was all thanks to those Austrade networking functions at the Sydney Olympics.'

Education is another area that has really benefited from closer Australian–Singaporean business links. After SAFTA was signed, Sean Riley, Australia's Senior Trade Commissioner in Singapore, was able to develop strong links with every major education exporter in town. 'We have Macquarie Graduate School of Management which has signed a deal with Raffles Campus, part of the Singapore Technologies group; the University of South Australia has run a strong advertising campaign in the *Straits Times*; and we recently had the Queensland University of Technology through. Vice chancellors are some of our more regular exporter visitors to the region,' he observed at the time. In addition, whilst the University of New South Wales (UNSW) has recently annouced that it will not be building its campus at Changi in Singapore due to issues concerning exposure to high levels of risk, it plans to deepen its existing partnerships with the National University of Singapore, Nanyang Technological University and several leading Singapore polytechnics. According to Pro Vice-Chancellor (International) Jennie Lang, the UNSW's links with Singapore are an important part of its strengthening Asia-Pacific strategy. 'We are building on long-term partnerships that have been developing for one to two decades now with our partner universities and polytechnics such as Singapore Polytechnic, Nanyang Polytechnic, Temasek Polytechnic and Ngee Ann Polytechnic, and increasing our involvement with our growing alumni chapters in Singapore and other parts of Asia. We plan to have a growing presence throughout the Southeast Asian region supported by our permanent UNSW office network in Asia (including China and India) where we are strengthening our connections and our brand.'

Sean Riley also observes that education overall is one of the professional services areas that will benefit from SAFTA well into the future. 'Our skill base, common language and close ties among young professionals will put us in a good position,' he said. In fact, Sean Riley, on a visit to Australia to publicise the importance of the Singapore market after the SARS outbreak, nominated education (both university and vocational), legal services, finance and architectural services as the SAFTA big winners from an Australian point of view.

Actually, education is a good note to finish on. With many of Singapore's government and business elite educated at Australian universities, the education export push from SAFTA will sow the seeds for stronger economic ties between Australia and Singapore in the future. As Raymond Lim himself points out: 'I am not the only Australian graduate around. Peter Ong, the permanent secretary of the Ministry of Transport, studied economics at the University of Adelaide as did Chia Tai Tee, one of the leading lights of the Government of Singapore Investment Corporation [GIC]. They call us the Adelaide mafia.' It wasn't just guys either. In fact, Lim Soo Hoon, the permanent secretary of the Public Service Division and Singapore's 'Woman of the Year' in 2006, was another Adelaide economics graduate. So educating Raymond and his colleagues in Australia has paid big dividends and people links will continue to prosper.

But maybe Singapore—and its famous Adelaide graduates—can let creativity bloom in a natural fashion, just like in the fair city of Adelaide. In the 1970s, South Australia's flamboyant and socially progressive premier Don Dunstan set up the Adelaide Festival of Arts and other cultural activities in the airport economist's home town. Despite its small size, Adelaide became a pacesetter for the rest of the nation, and its festivals and creative events (like the famous Fringe Festival) attracted international attention and have since been exported to other cities wanting their creative life to flourish. No creativity classes were needed then nor any elaborate plans or social engineering. After all, building a creative economy isn't rocket science.

2 LOVE THY NEIGHBOUR? LIVING WITH ASEAN

As they used to say on Sesame Street, *'Who are the people in your neighbourhood?' In Australia's case it's the Pacific nations, New Zealand, Papua New Guinea and the Association of Southeast Asian Nations (ASEAN). In fact, Australia and New Zealand are each currently negotiating a free trade agreement with the ASEAN states. So who makes up this region of ten countries and 550 million plus people? And how important are they to Australia? The airport economist investigates.*

IN BETWEEN ONE of ASEAN's richest members, Singapore, and one of its poorest, Vietnam, the airport economist decided to take a look at the 'middle income' developing countries of ASEAN. Many of these countries were hit hard by the Asian financial crisis in 1997–99 and the dotcom crash of 2001, so seeing how they were faring on their roads to recovery and on their aspirational journeys to join the ranks of the richer countries of Asia seemed a good idea.

But first, a bit of history. ASEAN was formed in 1967 by Singapore, Malaysia, Thailand, Indonesia and the Philippines. The original ASEAN-5 were later joined by Brunei, Vietnam, Laos, Cambodia and Burma to make double figures. Whilst originally a defence pact, ASEAN has grown

11

to become an important regional grouping on economic, trade, defence, security and development issues. ASEAN is very important to Australia as, according to Austrade research, over one-third of Australia's 44,000 exporters sell to ASEAN nations. In fact, ASEAN is likely to become even more important to Australia as a regional free trade area between Australia and New Zealand (through the Closer Economic Relations (CER) agreement) and ASEAN is currently being negotiated. This is big news as the ASEAN door has been shut to Australia in the past. A link with the ASEAN bloc would be significant as the region's GDP itself is worth almost US$862 billion (A$1150 billion), and the association has already announced deals with China (to be phased in by 2010) and Japan (by 2012). In fact, if a CER–ASEAN regional area was created through ASEAN's other expanded agreements, by 2026 we could see a regional trade area stemming from Hokkaido in northern Japan all the way south to Invercargill on the last bus stop to the South Pole.

Turtle Beach—Malaysia revisited

The first stop for the airport economist is Malaysia—just over 'the causeway' from Singapore—a small country of around the same population as Australia's where I had first travelled to in the mid-1980s. After visiting my brain-charged Singaporean friends, I headed by train up to Kuala Lumpur and Butterworth, the railway stop next to Penang. I had always wanted to visit Penang, one of Adelaide's 'sister cities', since seeing newspaper photos of then South Australian premier Don Dunstan driving Adele Koh, his Malaysian-born wife, in a pedal car during 'Penang Week' in Adelaide. In my backpack on that trip was a novel about Malaysia called *Turtle Beach* by Australian author Blanche d'Alpuget, the title inspired by the giant turtles that lay their eggs on the beaches of east coast Malaysia, a major tourist attraction.

When the airport economist first ventured to Kuala Lumpur he slept in a furniture factory in the old inner-city suburb of Sentul. The factory was owned by the father of one of my university friends, Ow Wai Cheng, who was typical of Malaysia's industrious Chinese community. Sentul was then a principally Indian suburb and Wai Cheng and I would dodge sacred cows as we made our way 'home' to the factory (to which the Ow family's living quarters were attached).

On my return twenty years later, Sentul and indeed the whole of Malaysia are different places. The cows are no more and gleaming skyscrapers—such as the Petronas Towers—dominate the modern downtown area of Kuala Lumpur. In addition, the east coast of Malaysia is now known for its mining ventures as well as the turtles that Blanche d'Alpuget wrote about. An Australian company, Grange Resources, has announced an A$400 million joint venture. This is welcome as Australia's foreign investment in Malaysia had been thin on the ground. According to James Wise, Australia's High Commissioner in Kuala Lumpur, 'It's been pretty much one-way traffic. Malaysians invest heavily in Australia, but with the exception of BlueScope Steel, Leightons, Ansell and CSR Building Products, we've been spread pretty thin. This new project by Grange Resources is most welcome here,' he says. Peter Kane, Australia's Trade Commissioner to KL, agrees: 'There's a steady stream of small and medium players coming through to Malaysia and the trading relationship is strong. However, investment tends to be centred on the usual suspects in corporate Australia.'

What are the reasons for the lack of Australian commercial interest in Malaysia? One reason could be that in our rush to China, many ASEAN nations missed out. Another could be that there have been occasionally frosty relations between the two nations, especially when long-standing prime minister Dr Mahathir Mohamad clashed with Australian prime minister Paul Keating over the merits of Asia-Pacific Economic Cooperation (APEC) in the early 1990s. However, whatever the state of Australian–Malaysian diplomacy, the people-links between Australia and Malaysia have remained strong. Throughout this time Malaysians kept sending their children to be educated at Australian universities, and some unis—like Monash, for example—set up campuses in Malaysia itself. As a result, many Australian students (such as the airport economist) made friends with Malaysians and subsequently visited the country.

In addition, the future forging of a Malaysia–Australia Free Trade Agreement (MAFTA) may do much to build stronger investment ties to match the trade flows. The Australian exporters who already sell to Malaysia could well build a foundation for further investment, joint ventures and strategic alliances. Healthcare, education and financial services are areas where more Australian businesses will partake in Malaysia's economic development. With incomes rising in Malaysia, more and better education will be demanded. Australian healthcare providers are likely to follow the success of Australian educational institutions and establish a presence in Malaysia. In addition, collaborative projects, such as the Grange Resources investment, will form part of an Australian expansion into Malaysia.

This surge of economic activity is all very welcome, but amongst it all let's hope there is still room for those giant turtles to lay their eggs on Turtle Beach.

The Thais that bind

The next stop after Malaysia is Bangkok. Thailand has been a good friend of Australia's—particularly at crucial times in our relationship with our other ASEAN neighbours. For example, in 1993, at the time of the APEC Leaders' Summit in Seattle when prime ministers Mahathir and Keating were clashing via the international media, an important intervention was made on behalf of Australia. Dr Supachai Panitchpakdi, the deputy prime minister of Thailand, made it clear to a high-level trade conference in Melbourne that Australia was an important part of the Asia-Pacific region and that Thailand regarded Australia as a key economic ally and good friend. The intervention of Dr Supachai helped Australia forge ahead in improving trade relations with Asia—particularly with ASEAN nations—and sent a strong message to the region about Thailand's leadership creden-tials in trade policy.

Over a decade and a half has passed and Thailand is still demonstrating its importance as a key economic ally of Australia. Australia has signed a free trade agreement with Thailand (known as the Thailand–Australia Free Trade Agreement, or TAFTA) and Australia and Thailand have developed strong cultural and commercial relationships.

So, from an Australian point of view, why Thailand? When the airport economist first visited Thailand in 1985, after staying within the comforts of university friends and family in Singapore and Malaysia, Bangkok was quite confronting. On arrival by train to Bangkok station from Butterworth/Penang, many local shysters and con men attempted to befriend and show me the sights of their city. Thankfully I was saved by a government employee from the Thai tourist agency, who took me around Bangkok for a week and not only allowed me to stay with him (or, rather, at each of his many girlfriends' houses), but also managed to get me into every major tourist attraction in the city and surrounds. So what was the catch? There was no catch. He was just a warm, generous person who was very proud of his city, his country and his culture. There were no hang-ups about foreigners or European colonists; the Thais could rely on their own traditions.

Of course, I was struck then by how poor Bangkok was, but on returning twenty years later I find significant economic progress has been made despite that baht devalu-ation which started the Asian financial crisis of 1997–99.

On my first visit since the 1980s, I asked Miles Kupa, Australia's Ambassador to the Kingdom of Thailand, about the country's economic strengths. 'Thailand is one of the best-performing economies in Southeast Asia,' he explained. 'It is second only to Indonesia in the region in terms of size, and the Thai economy, along with South Korea, bounced back quickly from the 1997–99 financial crisis. Thailand and Australia's trade patterns will complement each other well.' Ambassador Kupa is on his third posting in Thailand and is amazed by the changes that have occurred since the late 1970s. 'The Thais, of course, have a strong and proud culture, but are able to graft on all the advantages of modern global economies. The capacity to blend the two is very impressive.'

So how is Australia gaining from the trade agreement with Bangkok? According to Australia's lead negotiator, Justin Brown, Australia could find opportunities in a range of sectors including agribusiness, processed food, steel, auto components and pharmaceuticals. Australia's Senior Trade Commissioner in Bangkok, Cameron Macmillan, also thinks that Australian service exporters—in areas such as legal, architectural and engineering services—would have much to gain from the FTA. 'We have a strong Australian services presence in Bangkok, with law firms such as Minter Ellison and architectural firms like Wood Bagot,' he observes. 'These knowledge-based service exporters use Bangkok's strategic position as a "hub" to Laos, Cambodia and Vietnam. This enhances Thailand's position as a key trade partner for Australia in services.' In engineering, Graham Storah of Port Adelaide's Australian Submarine Corporation, whose overseas office is located in Bangkok, says: 'There are so many opportunities for Australian companies in this country—our engineering skills and know-how are greatly respected and Aussies are well-liked by the Thais.'

From a Thai point of view, TAFTA will help Thai agricultural and manufacturing exports to Australia. Dr Nilsuwan Leelarasamee emphasised the complementary nature of Australian–Thai trade. 'The types of fruit and vegetables that Thailand grows in a mainly tropical climate cannot be found in Australia. At the same time, Australia has many goods that Thailand cannot produce. It's a similar story in manufacturing.'

So, it seems the Australia–Thailand relationship is in a strong position and being further enhanced by the free trade agreement, while our personal links with Thailand remain solid at the highest level since Dr Supachai's firm support for Australia a decade or so ago. In turn, Dr Supachai became Director-General of the World Trade Organization with the strong support of Australia. In fact, given Dr Supachai's support of Australia and former deputy prime minister Tim Fischer's love of all things Thai, perhaps we should consider a football match—the Supachai–Fischer Cup—under the auspices of the Asian Football Confederation, Football Federation Australia and the Football Association of Thailand. This would keep things bubbling between our two nations as democracy returns to Thailand and allow many more things both Thai and Australian to flourish.

Indonesia's recovery—will there be a boom-boom for Bambang?

Next stop is Indonesia, one of the world's most populous nations, which sits right on Australia's doorstep. Indonesia has always played a role in Australia's consciousness. However, despite being close neighbours, Australians and Indonesians don't really know much about each other. Could a barnstorming trip around Jakarta help? Or would I just be looking at the tip of the iceberg in understanding the archipelago?

When I think of Indonesia, I often remember the 1982 Peter Weir film *The Year of Living Dangerously* (one of Mel Gibson's early movies) about the coup against Indonesia's founding president, Sukarno, in the 1960s. However, the year 1997 was also the year of living dangerously—economically speaking—in Indonesia. In 1997, Indonesia was one of the major skittles to fall during the Asian financial crisis, with institutional collapse and the eventual downfall of the long-running regime of former president Suharto. The International Monetary Fund (IMF) was called in to deal with the financial rescue operation and many international economic observers—including Australia's then deputy governor of the Reserve Bank, Stephen Grenville, who was a diplomat in Jakarta before joining the central bank—were instrumental in helping Indonesia put together a policy package of reform and recovery.

However, it is now over a decade since those fateful days of 1997 and local pundits and officials report that things have improved for the country. Why is this so? First, I was told, Indonesia's economic performance has drastically improved. Second, many home-grown Indonesian policy-makers have come to the fore of economic reconstruction and recovery. And third, Indonesia has become a fully fledged democracy under President Susilo Bambang Yudhoyono (known as 'Bambang' or 'SBY').

Indonesia has also been developing stronger capacity in economic policy advice. In fact, Dr Sri Mulyani Indrawati, the Indonesian Minister of Finance, was recently awarded *Euromoney*'s world finance minister of the year (an award won by former Australian treasurer Paul Keating in 1984). Many of her advisers are Australian-trained with strong links to our academic and business communities.

But has the strengthening of Indonesian democracy—and, for that matter, economic policy advice—changed perceptions of the Indonesian investment climate? On the numbers alone, University of Indonesia economist Dr Chatib Basri points out that Indonesia's investment-to-GDP ratio is actually higher than several other ASEAN economies such as Malaysia. However, it may be the case that a benign Indonesian investment climate is 'necessary but not sufficient' for further development. For instance, supply-side 'capacity constraints' are also hindering development, with infrastructure and tax reform seen as key responses to advance economic reform. In addition, some major incentives on the institutional side—such as enforceability of contract and rule of law—are seen by both Indonesian and international commentators alike as areas that need improvement.

Which particular sectors are ripe for Australian investment? Banking and telecommunications are, in many ways, seen as the jewels in the crown of Indonesia's economy. There has been a widespread rationalisation of banks in Indonesia, and fewer problems with non-performing loans. Both the ANZ (with its investment in Panin Bank) and the Commonwealth (with its wholly owned subsidiary PT Bank Commonwealth) entered into joint venture arrangements prior to the financial crisis in 1997. They are now benefiting from taking a long-term perspective and have profitable businesses in Indonesia. In addition, telecommunications is going from strength to strength with the growth of Indonesia's young population. However, there is still some microeconomic reform needed in traditional extractive sectors such as mining and forestry in light of the challenges of climate change.

And then of course there's the IMF. Stephen Schwartz, Country Director for Indonesia, believes that the country has achieved significant macroeconomic stability, with economic growth now in the 5 to 6 per cent range, public debt to GDP at manageable levels and a build-up of reserves. In fact, on the back of this improved macroeconomic and fiscal performance, Indonesia paid back its IMF loan four years ahead of schedule which, according to Schwartz, is a great source of pride for the Indonesian people. This has also made life a little easier for IMF officials in Jakarta after its sometimes unpopular role in 1997. 'It's very different nowadays, I can openly tell people where I work—except, perhaps, for taxi drivers,' he says.

So more than ten years after the events of 1997, Indonesia is seemingly back on its feet with an open democracy and a commitment to economic reform. But further substantial institutional reforms are required to help attract sustainable international investment. Let's hope that Indonesia's economic recovery continues and that future IMF officials in Indonesia can even tell taxi drivers what they do for a living.

A Thriller in Manila—grappling with the Philippines

The final stop on the whistlestop tour of the main ASEAN economies is the Philippines, an enigmatic nation that combines Spanish, American, Japanese and local influences as a result of many years of colonisation and invasion. The Philippines first came to the airport economist's attention in 1975, during the Marcos regime, when the country was host to one of the greatest sports spectacles of all time: the world heavyweight boxing title fight between the legendary Muhammad 'The Greatest' Ali and 'Smokin' Joe' Frazier. Both fighters endured incredible levels of pain over fifteen arduous rounds of heavy-duty punishment. This famous bout—the third Ali–Frazier epic—was dubbed 'The Thrilla in Manila', following on from 'The Rumble in the Jungle' in Zaire (where Ali famously regained his title from the more highly fancied George Foreman).

'The Rumble in the Jungle' was the subject of an Academy Award-winning documentary, *When We Were Kings*, whilst 'The Thrilla in Manila' was also memorable to many Australian audiences for TV comic Norman Gunston's famous pre-fight interview with Muhammad Ali. Ali—ever the showman—seemingly became angrier with Gunston as the interview progressed, even madder than he had been with Joe Frazier and George Foreman. As always with Ali, he performed as well for the TV cameras as he did in the ring.

Thirty years on, a heavyweight bout of a different sort has been occupying the Philippine archipelago but this time, during the airport economist's first visit to Manila, the punches are being thrown in the courtroom rather than the boxing ring. After many rounds, lasting years rather than minutes, and numerous appeals the Supreme Court in Manila has finally allowed foreign companies to take a stake in the mining industry in the Philippines. This will open the door for foreign investors in a major untapped resource sector.

'This is great news for Australia,' explains Australia's Senior Trade Commissioner in Manila, Alan Morrell. 'It will really give investors some certainty and there have been many mineral deposits left dormant whilst the legal argy-bargy took place. We hope many Australian mining companies will now take a fresh look at the Philippines,' he says.

Indeed, the impact of the Supreme Court decision could be significant for the Philippines. Peter Wallace, an Australian expatriate businessman and well-known media commentator in Manila, believes the expansion of the mining industry could really bring benefit to the national economy. In a speech to the influential Wallace Business Forum, he said: 'The country's potential mineral wealth is estimated at US$840 billion. We can expect exploration to rise by US$200 million with capital investment of US$3.2 billion for new projects within the next five to ten years. From that we'll expect production to increase to US$3.7 billion and create about 10,000 jobs.'

Of course, the Supreme Court proceedings did not stop companies in *mining-related* industries doing business in the Philippines. For instance, Leighton Contractors have been involved in mining construction and equipment, along with some smaller suppliers. Michael Templeton, Leightons' Finance and Administration Manager, has been active in the Philippines and sees this decision as a good sign. 'The Philippines has really been underrated and off the radar screen. This new legal development is coming at an opportune time,' he explains. Templeton is a pillar of the Australian expatriate community in Manila and is active in the Philippine Rugby Football Union.

However, according to Austrade Manila, whilst mining was on hold pending the legal battles, some other sectors have been more active, including the usual Australian suspects in the modern export game like food and beverages (including wine), IT and communications, but also others like education and financial services.

In the wine industry, a number of mainly South Australian entrepreneurs are succeeding well on both price and quality grounds. Brett Tolhurst, of the famous South Australian wine family, runs a very successful online wine club in the affluent Makati City district of Manila. 'It takes a while to get established, but I found the Philippines a good place to do business after working in Australia and Hong Kong. They know their wines well, and Australia has a good reputation despite the strong links of this country with Spain and the USA,' he says. Growth in wine sales is being accompanied by strong performance in gourmet foods, helped by Australia's reputation as a 'clean and green' supplier of fresh produce. According to Australia's Trade Commissioner for the Philippines, Dan Williams, 'The supermarket shelves of Makati are stacked with Aussie foodstuffs and we have over fifty clients in Manila involved in the food industry.'

In information technology, the Philippines is proving to be a strong market for telecommunications. The Wallace Business Forum estimates that 'There are over 67 call centres in the Philippines, employing over 40,000 people. At least 19 international companies have centralized backroom operations in the country including P&G, AIG and HSBC.' The fact that English is widely spoken along with the Filipinos' reputation for friendly and efficient customer service are considered key reasons for these investments.

In addition, global mobile phone technology sales have been boosted by the Filipino interest in communications gadgets and use of text messaging, in particular. According to Peter Laurence, Chief Financial Officer for Smart Telecommunications: 'The Filipinos are constantly texting each other. Why? It's simply so much cheaper than talking direct by a ratio of 7:1, so all over bars and restaurants in Manila you see plenty of locals busily making arrangements and texting each other on their mobiles.'

In fact, the airport economist was surprised at all the texting in Manila because the Filipino people are so gregarious and all seem to be great singers and entertainers. It's often said in Asian workplaces: get the Singaporeans to do the accounts, but make sure the Filipinos run (and, of course, perform at) the Christmas party! The knack of Filipinos to stand out was evident when the airport economist was on an Asia-Pacific delegation run by the United States Informational Agency (known in some circles as the 'CIA scholarship') in 1994. During the trip, we visited many major cities across the United States to improve US–Asian trade relations and, in each city, the local Asia Society put on a lunch or dinner (or an unreasonably early breakfast in the less civilised cities). And at all events, in all cities, the Asia Society was run by Filipinos— or, to be exact, *Filipinas*, as the Philippines clearly produces some strong, lively and outgoing womenfolk. So I guess that 7:1 cost ratio must be driving all that texting behaviour in the Philippines, as even a country of extroverts knows the importance of relative prices and can spot a bargain when they see one!

According to Professor Emilio T. Antonio Jr, an economist at the University of Asia and The Pacific (UAP), all this demand for communication services in the Philippines is driven by the large number of expatriate Filipinos working outside the country. Professor Antonio explains that expatriate remittances are a 'major source of national income for the Philippines and they also form a major portion of demand for communications within the archipelago itself'. This large offshore Filipino community also increases demand for transport services. As Honeybee Hubahib, Qantas Country Manager for the Philippines, attests, 'We are constantly pushing for more flights between Sydney and Manila, with links to Melbourne, Perth and Brisbane too.'

In financial services, the head of ANZ for the Philippines, Johnny Co, says that Australian banks have a good reputation in the Manila financial sector. 'During the Asian financial crisis in 1997–99, the Australian institutions stuck with Southeast Asia through thick and through thin. As a result, there is a lot of goodwill throughout the region,' he explains.

So what does the future hold for Australia's trade with the Philippines? According to Alan Morrell: 'Of course, the Supreme Court decision will remove impediments to mining investment and that will really help on the export revenue side. But we expect smaller players to do well too, given the Philippines' bustling retail sector and interest in telecommunications, travel and emerging services sectors.'

Indeed, the evidence backs up Morrell's intuition. Recent Austrade research suggests there are over 1400 Australian businesses exporting to the Philippines, which compares favourably with richer markets such as France and Italy. In addition, surveys from Sensis show that the Philippines has been quite an active market for small- and medium-sized enterprises (SMEs), with about 4 per cent of all Australian SMEs exporting there (compared to 3 per cent for Thailand, which has a free trade agreement with Australia to boot). This just shows that you don't have to be the business equivalent of a Muhammad Ali or a Smokin' Joe Frazier to succeed in the Filipino market.

3 MOTORCYCLE DIARIES

Why are there so many motorcyclists in Vietnam? Have they been inspired by Che Guevara or Ho Chi Minh? The airport economist investigates this newest 'Asian tiger' from south to north.

IT'S THIRTY YEARS since the fall of Saigon and Australian trade guru Tim Gauci is riding a motorcycle on a steamy Vietnamese morning, looking more like a modern-day Che Guevara than a Ho Chi Minh.

The (pre-revolutionary) Guevara undertook a famous ride across South America as a young man in the 1950s, and his journal entries from the time were subsequently made into a book and the hit movie *Motorcycle Diaries*. Gauci, who by day serves as Austrade's Senior Trade Commissioner in Hanoi, is crossing the country with a group of Vietnamese and French motorcyclist friends. Like Guevara, he is a sharp observer of the evolving society around him. 'It's amazing how fast the country has changed. What were rice paddies are now hubs of business activity. Even in the poorer rural areas, the Vietnamese are natural entrepreneurs,' he observes.

And Gauci is certainly not alone on the road—the airport economist can barely cross the road in Ho Chi Minh City (formerly Saigon) without finding himself engulfed in a rugby scrum of Vietnamese two-wheelers. There has been a boom in motorcycles in Vietnam that has become symbolic of Vietnamese aspirations to be a modern consumer society. According to Vietnamese journalist Nguyen Ngoc Son, 'To some extent, the motorbike market is a microcosm for high-end consumption trends in Vietnam. In the early 1990s, people were proud of owning a basic Honda Dream motorbike, but attitudes have changed in recent years. With the emergence of higher-end Honda models like the @ and the Dylan, which retail at around $5000, the sturdy Dream has become rather ordinary.' And the resulting traffic snarls from all these bikes are compounded by the increasing number of buses and cars on the road. From Lada to Mercedes Benz, Vietnam's roads are starting to resemble downtown Bangkok. It seems that the emerging Vietnamese middle-class is becoming tired of battling the elements on two wheels and opting for increasingly affordable four-wheeled transport.

The expansion of the consumer market and the rise in aspirations of the Vietnamese people are reflective of their economic success as a 'transition tiger'. This gradual change from a communist country to a market-orientated consumer society—more like China than the 'short sharp shock' experience of Russia—has taken many economists by surprise. As Swedish economist Stefan de Vylder wrote: 'Compared to other countries undergoing a transition from central planning to a market economy, Vietnam's process of economic reform (*doi moi*, or 'renewal') is remarkably successful. The rate of economic growth has been high for almost 15 years, and poverty is estimated to have been reduced from well over 50 per cent of the population in the early 1990s to around one-third at the end of the decade.'

And you ain't seen nothing yet! Nguyen Ngoc Son predicts that 'Although Vietnam is still fighting poverty in remote and mountainous areas, the country's 7 per cent growth rate over the last few years and foreign remittances of over US$3 billion per year are sure to create a burgeoning middle-class in the big cities.'

In their ambition to transform the Vietnamese economy and meet the needs of the aspiring urban middle-class, the country's authorities have become more open to trade and foreign investment than ever before. Foreign companies have been made welcome—even from the United States and Australia, despite the events of thirty years ago. Around the same time that the airport economist was in Vietnam, the World Bank President, Robert Zoellick, in his former capacity as US Deputy Secretary of State, was also visiting Hanoi and Ho Chi Minh City. The former United States Trade Representative made much of the improved trade links between his country and Vietnam after a cold war–like freeze in relations following the fall of Saigon in 1975. He comments that times have improved between the two former enemies: 'Since the US–Vietnam Bilateral Trade Agreement took effect in December 2001, trade between the two countries has expanded considerably. Vietnamese exports to the US have grown to US$4 or 5 billion a year, while US exports to Vietnam stand at about US$1.3 billion a year . . . Trade and investment can be a win–win venture. We know how important this is to Vietnam's development. We want to be able to see Vietnam develop and become a greater force in the world economy.' Zoellick has played an important role in helping restore economic relations with Hanoi, which has proved to be a tricky task given the influence of some Vietnam veterans groups in the United States who abhor contact with the Southeast Asian republic.

And in the case of Australia, another Vietnam War combatant, issues of trade are certainly replacing those of conflict. Australia has been a major contributor to Vietnam in terms of development aid—the construction of the My Thuan Bridge in the Mekong Delta, an AusAID-funded $90 million infrastructure project which opened in 2000, is testament to that—but there's increasing action on the commercial front too as Vietnam's economy has looked up. By the middle of the noughties, merchandise trade between Australia and Vietnam had increased to more than A$4 billion, with services trade totalling A$630 million with Vietnam becoming Australia's seventeenth largest merchandise trading partner, whilst Australia had become Vietnam's seventh largest merchandise trading partner. Australia was also Vietnam's seventeenth largest foreign investor. Australia's corporate presence is made up of all the usual household names, such as ANZ Bank, BlueScope Steel, QBE Insurance, Fosters, the Commonwealth Bank (trading as CMG) and Visy Packaging. But there are also new areas emerging in professional services, engineering, tourism and education. For example, the World Bank and the Asian Development Bank have been active in working with visiting Australian education providers in Vietnam such as Melbourne's RMIT University and Brisbane's Griffith University. Whilst in Hanoi, the airport economist met a large Australian university delegation led by former Queensland deputy premier, the late Tom Burns. Burns, a long-standing observer and friend of Vietnam, said that the links would only strengthen between Australia and Vietnam: 'Vietnam cast such a shadow over Australian public life that it remains part of our consciousness. Let's hope that we can use our influence to better the lives of the ordinary Vietnamese people, who suffered so much for many decades.'

But along with the well-known blue-chip corporate players, there are a large number of Australian small- and medium-sized enterprises exporting to Vietnam as well. According to Austrade research, around 1029 Australian businesses export to Vietnam with 110 Australian companies actually based there. Many of these companies are in the south and are a result of Vietnamese expatriates investing in their country of origin. According to James Myers, Australia's Trade Commissioner, in Ho Chi Minh City, 'There are about 300,000 overseas Vietnamese in Australia and increasingly they are looking to invest back home. As a result, there's a real buzz here in Ho Chi Minh City.' Myers has also noticed the strong presence of Australians in general in Vietnam. 'There are around 6000 Aussies in Ho Chi Min City alone, but many are also looking to the regions where there are plenty of opportunities in agribusiness and tourism-related infrastructure,' he says.

Back in Australia, Duyet Le Van, a leading member of the Vietnamese–NSW Chamber of Commerce, agrees. 'We have seen far more interest in Vietnam from Australia, particularly after the visit of Prime Minister Phan van Khai and fifty Vietnamese business leaders in 2005. I expect that as Vietnam grows and needs Australian skills and experience, we will see more investment from our members here in Australia,' he said in an interview with the airport economist in Sydney in 2006.

Vietnam's move to join the World Trade Organization (WTO) in 2007, which Australia strongly supported, was a landmark decision in its quest to become a more open, market-orientated economy. Openness to trade has really helped Vietnam. According to the Australian Embassy's Michael Growder: 'Trade is worth some 140 to 150 per cent of Vietnam's GDP with both exports and imports growing rapidly at around 20 per cent per annum. The US has been a key export destination for Vietnam and China a key source of imports.'

The WTO decision was loudly applauded by the World Bank. Whilst in Hanoi, the airport economist visited the bank's Country Director, Klaus Rohland, who explained that 'For developing countries like Vietnam, wanting access for their goods and services, joining the WTO is the best protection against protectionism.'

However, Patrick Stringer, Gauci's successor in Hanoi and a long-time observer of Vietnam, is still concerned that there is much further to go in Vietnam to improve the lot of the poor, particularly in rural areas. 'In the 1980s, people were starving in the streets of Hanoi. Nowadays things are much better, although there's a big gap between the north and south, and the countryside and the city,' he says. The evidence supports his observations. It's a real 'tale of two cities' as far as Hanoi and Ho Chi Minh City go. Per capita income in Ho Chi Minh City is US$1500 per annum compared to US$1000 for Hanoi. In addition, there's a 'bright lights, big city' phenomenon going on with Vietnam's young population; after all, per capita income is only around US$500 in rural areas, and this is where three-quarters of the Vietnamese people still live. Although there's little doubt, given the evidence, that keeping the country closed to trade and eschewing the *doi moi* reforms would have made their plight much worse.

For now, let's say good morning, Vietnam, and hope that Vietnamese economic fortunes and living standards continue to improve. If so, we can expect many more motor-cyclists—with bikes of greater power and quality—following Tim Gauci's example of travelling through the Vietnamese countryside in the years ahead.

4 SHANGHAI OF THE TIGER

What has Swan Lake *got in common with the Sydney Swans? The airport economist watches the very first all-China Australian Rules football derby between the Shanghai Tigers and the Beijing Bombers and then is off to a performance of* Swan Lake *in Shanghai by the Australian Ballet. Next the airport economist finds Australian influences in all sorts of nooks and crannies, well beyond the rich, coastal cities of China's eastern seaboard.*

WHEN YOU THINK of the great modern football rivalries, it's usually Essendon–Collingwood, Richmond–Carlton and, in more modern times, West Coast–Fremantle (the 'Western Derby') and Adelaide–Port Adelaide (the 'Showdown' in South Australia) that come to mind. However, on a recent visit to China I discover another great rivalry in the mix when the Shanghai and Beijing Aussie Rules footy clubs play off in the All-China AFL derby at Shanghai's Jinqiao Pudong stadium, known as 'the MCG of China'.

The Shanghai Tigers Australian Rules Football Club is largely made up of Australian expatriates, with a few Americans, Kiwis, Brits and local Chinese players roped in. Whilst mainly a social club, the Tigers also play matches and train once a week. According to Shanghai Tigers President Nigel

Goode, 'We have forty members on our books and, apart from the matches, we also conduct coaching clinics for young kids and undertake community work.' The Tigers also play a useful role in networking for Aussie expatriates on both a social and commercial level. 'It's great for Aussies that are new to town,' Nigel explains. 'I wish there was something like this six years ago when I arrived. It's great for making business contacts and to meet new friends as well.'

The Shanghai Tigers is basically run by Goode, Richard David and the well-known McGregor clan. Father Jock McGregor has headed the ANZ Bank in China for the past eight years, and is legendary in local business circles. Mother Vicki McGregor is the organiser supremo and the backbone of the club's events and charity work. And son Ross McGregor is the club's co-founder and the driving force of the AFL competition in China. As Ross says, 'We aspire to be like the strong AFL clubs in Singapore, Hong Kong and throughout Southeast Asia, and the All-China grudge matches against Beijing are a good springboard for further development.'

One of Ross McGregor's recent initiatives was to bring over several past and present Richmond players—including Greg Stafford, Mark Chaffey, Patrick Bowden and Ray Hall.

Greg Stafford, the former Sydney Swans ruckman who recently retired as a Richmond player, enjoyed the tour and was really impressed by China. 'We have a pretty short off-season in footy before pre-season training starts, so it is important to expand your horizons and China has been a real eye-opener for the boys,' he says. Stafford, a skilled speaker and media performer, is also looking at a future post-football business career in building and construction, and has his eye on the Chinese market. 'I'm told they build the equivalent of a city the size of Brisbane each year, so the pace of construction is just mind-boggling,' he comments.

The Shanghai Tigers don't just do it for premiership glory and the odd pub crawl for Aussie expats, it seems, and when

I was in Shanghai the Tigers held a major fundraising dinner for the Half the Sky foundation, which manages orphanages in the cities of Guilin and Chengdu, in southern and western China respectively. Half the Sky is a well-respected organisation that concentrates its resources on the emotional development of Chinese infants before they are adopted out. In fact, the airport economist's own daughter, Yun Shi, is from Half the Sky in Guilin. Given that Yun Shi is just over three years old, we have very few disagreements—except she does think the Chinese exchange rate should remained fixed for the foreseeable future!

According to Michael Wadley, a Shanghai-based Australian lawyer and club supporter, 'Many of the Shanghai Tigers have adopted Chinese children or have friends and family who have done so. In many ways, the club is not just about meeting fellow expats, it's about contributing to Chinese society as well.'

The Shanghai Tigers are just one aspect of a strong Australian face in China. On the airport economist's first visit, I noticed South Australia's Beerenberg jam on the Dragon Airlines flight from Hong Kong to Shanghai, Fosters neon signs on the freeway from the airport, an Australian-made GPS meter in my taxi (proudly shown to me by the driver), Jacob's Creek wine in the hotel bar and the ABC's Asia-Pacific channel on the television screen of my hotel room. All before I'd even unpacked! In Beijing, I even met a group of people who were raising corporate sponsorship for the wombat enclosure at the Beijing Zoo! In fact, the airport economist suggested that we export 'Fatso the Wombat' of Roy and HG's *The Dream*, their late-night TV program that was such a big hit during the Sydney Olympics in 2000. It would be a nice symmetry given the close links between the Sydney Olympics in 2000 and the Beijing Games in 2008.

But Australia's presence in China is not confined to the big modern coastal cities like Beijing, Shanghai and Guangzhou. The 'second- and third-tier cities' such as

Chongqing, Dalian, Qingdao, Xi'an, Kunming, Wuhan, Nanning and Chengdu are keen to generate economic growth and attract infrastructure investment in airports, freeways, factories, offices and apartments for their growing populations. And remember these regional centres are not country towns. The Chongqing region is estimated to have 12 million inhabitants, Wuhan 7 million, Nanning 6 million and Chengdu 5 million.

The rise of the interior is also good news for Australian exporters. According to Peter Ironmonger, Australia's Trade Commissioner in Shanghai, 'In many ways, the PRD [Pearl River Delta] represented the first wave of modernisation, with the Shanghai–Pudong region being the second wave. Now the interior and the western regions are looking to follow the coastal areas in terms of their own economic development. This will provide great opportunities for Australian companies involved in infrastructure, construction, architecture and environmental design.'

For example in architecture, Australian firm Hassell has won big contracts in Chongqing. Peter Duncan, Hassell's principal, says that there are benefits in chasing work in 'second-tier' cities, outside the big three: 'You get great access to decision-makers in Chongqing, and relative to places like Shanghai and Beijing, it's a pretty open field. Every man and his dog are in Shanghai, with the Americans, Europeans and the rest of the world there competing for the work.'

Indeed, Hassell is not alone. Many architects, environmental design companies and town-planners are doing well in regional China as well as picking up the high-profile Olympic-based projects in Beijing. This indicates that Australia's export base to China is broadening, with professional services and niche manufacturers joining the resource houses and blue-chip corporates. In fact, according to the latest data, more Australian companies export to China than ever before. In comparing Australian exporter destinations by company since 1989, China has clearly been the chartbuster. According to research prepared by Austrade and Sensis, 20 per cent of all small- and medium-sized exporters sell to the China market—a figure that doubled in only two years.

So why is Australia so well-placed?

The first reason is Sino-Australian diplomacy. Australia has been regarded as a good friend of China since Canberra's recognition of the People's Republic in 1972, a feeling further enhanced by Australia's support for China's entry into the World Trade Organization in 2001. The bilateral relationship is strong and this makes a real difference at all levels of government in China, whether it be central, provincial or local. For example, having a trade commissioner or ambassador accompanying an Australian company to meet a local official can go a long way when tendering for a contract, especially when Beijing has a favourable view of Australia.

Second, there is strong exporter support for closer economic ties with China. According to the majority of business surveys conducted in Australia, our exporters—both large and small—really are 'panda huggers', with bullish views about the China market on a consistent basis.

Third, as well as having trade interests that are complementary, Australian business skills are well-regarded. We are good at running large projects and have a strong professional service culture. This is consistent with recent global surveys demonstrating the current strength of the Australian 'brand'. For example, GMI-Anholt ranked Australia as the number one country brand in the world, meaning that Australians are regarded as being very good to work with and do business with.

Finally, there's the important role played by Chinese-Australians in facilitating trade between their countries. People like Jimmy Du, of Australian manufacturer Dynalite, whom the airport economist met in Shanghai, and Dr Dan Sun, of IBM China, who was educated in Australia, all provide natural links between Australia and China. According to Dan Sun, 'It's easy for me: I work for Australia, I was educated in Australia, and my son is in school there. Everyone is coming to Shanghai but I want to make sure Australian exporters also take advantage of the opportunities occurring all over China.' Dan Sun, a native of regional China himself (he hails from Kunming, a south-western city), has risen quickly up the corporate ranks after gaining an Australian education.

But is it all good news in China? Peter Osborne, Austrade's China Country Manager in Beijing, says that many exporters make the mistake of thinking that size is the only thing that matters. 'Many average Aussies think you just have to sell a pair of socks to everyone in China and "presto", you'll sell 1.3 billion pairs of socks just like that, but it's actually more complicated,' he explains. Osborne warns that intellectual property is still a big issue in China and that it is important to use official government channels to filter out any unscrupulous middleman who will commercially harm unsuspecting foreign businesspeople. 'With such a large market there are a lot of opportunities in China, but there are bad eggs as well, so government links are needed for your own protection,' Osborne says.

But let's get back to the footy. After celebrating with the Shanghai Tigers after their win, I noticed that the Shanghai–Beijing rivalry is just as intense if you veer from the AFL Swans to *Swan Lake*. As the footy players were squaring off, the Australian Ballet was holding a function to discuss Australian and Chinese contemporary dance at Shanghai's famous M on the Bund restaurant. The Australian Ballet's rendition of *Swan Lake* was part of a 'Celebrate Australia, Australian Style' programme being held throughout Shanghai, and it was at this event that the world-famous Chinese dancer Jin Xing commented on the 'sibling-city rivalry'. When she moved from Beijing to Shanghai, she recalled, it delighted Shanghai audiences but caused an outcry in Beijing cultural circles: 'They said, how could I move to "the other place"?' Australian artists in China are free from such cloistered cultural notions although, as Australian ballet legend Graeme Murphy comments, 'The Australian Ballet has strong links to Shanghai and we were one of the first dance companies to perform here after the Cultural Revolution.'

Clearly there is a great diversity of Australian input in Shanghai as Christopher Wright, Australia's Senior Trade Commissioner, explains: 'We have everything Australian from James Morrison to mandarins—known as the M & Ms. We also have a large number of prominent Australian expats in town, from Michelle Garnaut of M on the Bund, to Adelaide-born Steve Baker of the famous restaurant Mesa and the like.'

So whether it's the Swans or *Swan Lake* that takes your fancy, you'll find it all in Shanghai. And watch out for that Shanghai–Beijing rivalry—it leaves the Melbourne–Sydney tension for dead ... and given Shanghai's most recent Australian Rules victory over their northern rivals, we can expect to be hearing more about these 'Asian tigers' in years to come!

5 LOST IN TRANSLATION

Why do the Japanese still hold expos? And what is their obsession with almost human-like robots? At the Aichi Expo in Nagoya, the airport economist gets entertained by Tommy Emmanuel and taken in by some local impostors.

THE AIRPORT ECONOMIST'S first ever trip to Japan was in 1969 at the tender age of four. My father was undertaking a sabbatical at Keio University and a Japanese family (friends of my dad's academic colleagues) moved out of their place so we could stay there. This was amazing hospitality—especially given that we were a family of four kids and that our stay was for around six months in total.

Back then there were very few foreigners in Japan; the country had only just started to reach the living standards of the western world and was not very open to visitors. In 1969, few Japanese had been to Australia or even knew where it was, so an Australian four year old with ginger hair was stared at on the subway (more out of curiosity than any hostility).

There's no question what the highlight of Japan in 1969 was—for a four-year-old-boy, it was the bullet train (or *Shinkansen*) of course! My family took the bullet train to Osaka to visit the site of the forthcoming expo, which was

to be held in Japan's second largest city in 1970. The 1970
expo in Osaka was symbolic of how far Japan had come in the
world economically.

In 2005, the airport economist returned to Japan and
found himself at yet another expo, this time in Aichi prefec-
ture, centred around Japan's fourth largest city, Nagoya. The
modern expo, however, comes at a time when Japan is a
much more open society. After all, the Japanese people now
visit overseas countries regularly and in greater numbers. In
1970, only 200,000 Japanese travelled overseas annually
whilst now it is nearly 17 million. According to the Japanese
tourism authorities, Australia and Hawaii are consistently the
country's most popular overseas holiday destinations.

In fact, the original expos were held when international
travel was rare and the country exhibitions were the closest
people got to actually visiting other nations. But now, in an
age of international travel, what purpose do expos serve? In
some ways they are a marketing device—potential visitors can
get a feel for a country before selecting a place to holiday or
even study or work in. Many countries—particularly Australia
and New Zealand—really play up the tourism angle, and
Australia's efforts have worked well. According to Japanese
media outlets, the Australian pavilion at the 2005 expo was
rated in the top five of the 121 national displays.

However, expos also provide direct benefits in terms of
trade according to Phil Ingram, Australia's Senior Trade
Commissioner in Tokyo. 'Expos do attract more trade missions—like bees around a honeypot. We've seen an
extraordinary pick-up in the number of Australian missions
coming to Japan in areas such as biotech, automotive, environmental technology, food, sports and ICT,' he says.

Expos also highlight regions in Japan that otherwise
wouldn't get much profile. Denis Zolin, Australia's Senior
Trade Commissioner in the expo host city of Nagoya, says:
'Nagoya was once just perceived as a train stop between
Tokyo and Osaka, but the place is now booming. The hosting

of the expo here coupled with Toyota's decision to base its international headquarters in Nagoya is a real endorsement of the city.'

But is this expo-related trade activity indicative of Australia's overall trade relationship with Japan? Not really. The resource sector still dominates the relationship, according to Phil Ingram: 'Expos are good for niche players to get some profile. It helps broaden our perceptions of our export base.'

In fact, there are clearly a number of new influences that are helping to boost Australia's export outlook in the land of the rising sun. First, as the 1992 US election cliché goes, it's the economy, stupid. The overall macroeconomic environment in Japan is slowly improving. According to Bank of Tokyo-Mitsubishi economist Tatsuo Tanaka, 'Japan's economy is beginning to end its temporary lull, helped by firm domestic demand and recovering exports, with progress in global inventory adjustments.'

Second, there's the possibility of a new wave of reform on the back of the measures initiated by former Prime Minister Koizumi. 'Koizuminomics' has the potential to really open up the Japanese economy. According to seasoned Japan-watchers, in his early years Koizumi faced strong resistance to reform from within his own Liberal Democratic Party ranks, but his electoral appeal (including a stunning victory in 2005) gave the green light to continue his reform programme. Hopefully, his successors will attempt to emulate his success. They may not have his famous 'Elvis' hairstyle, but it would be great for both Japan and the rest of the world if they could continue some of his reform momentum.

Third, Japan's unique demographics are also creating export opportunities at both ends of the age scale that are particularly suited to Australia. At the young end of the market, surf exports are booming. According to the latest ABS data, Australia exports around $21 million worth of waterskis, surfboards and water sports equipment, with Japan

being the number one destination and accounting for
$8 million worth of exports. Ikuko Matsumoto, a Business
Development Manager with Austrade in Nagoya, says that
surfing is big in the central Japan region and many new
Australian companies are doing business there.

Young people are also creating opportunities for some
entrepreneurial Australian service exporters in the labour
market. Whilst Japan is often talked about as the land of the
greying sun because of is ageing population, there coexists
an influential younger generation with different attitudes to
travel, culture and work. This is particularly evident in the
labour market, where the Japanese tradition of 'salarymen'
working for the same company for life has been replaced by
the 'freeter' phenomenon, where causal employment and
ever-changing jobs and careers has up-ended the dynamics of
the Japanese work relationship. There has been debate about
the freeter concept. Some scholars have claimed it is the
choice of younger people not to be tied down to one employer
or one job, whilst many freeters themselves claim that they
would prefer more job security but cannot find permanent
positions because of the changing nature of work in Japan.
According to Tomoko Ichikawa, a business development
manager with Austrade Tokyo, the freeter trend is also a
consequence of changing family structures in Japan. 'Family
sizes are getting smaller and baby boomer parents often like
to have their kids at home. They are known as *amai* or "sweet"
in their attitudes towards their live-in adult children,' she
explains. This has allowed their off-spring to be more
'choosy' about their occupation and has greatly enhanced
their capacity to consume goods and services other than
housing.

However, the freeter phenomenon has opened up opportunities for Australian service exporters specialising in job
placement and career services. For example, Australian
Terrie Lloyd, President of Linc Media, has set up an online
recruiting company, DaiJob.com, aimed at 'freeter' job

seekers. He sees this as a boom market: 'Traditionally, Japan engineers society, but now Japanese society is opening up in a manner that is neither engineered or controlled.' The rise of the Internet, mobile phones and SMS messages, Lloyd believes, is 'setting up a whole new youth subculture based on the information revolution, which is more open to western influences than ever before'.

Then there's the other end of the scale. Grey power in Japan is doing its bit for our export account as well. Tourism, for instance, plays a big role. According to Nobutaka Ishikure, the Chief Industry Officer at Japan Airlines, 'We target three groups in our marketing—the YOLs (young office ladies), the OLs (office ladies) and the OBs (old boys). The OBs, or *jukunen*, are really important as they have time to spend in Australia on a range of leisure and educational activities. Their trips are longer as retirement frees them up for longer stays.' As a result, Japanese tourism is more than a quick bus tour and a lightning visit to the Gold Coast. Retirees are taking their time, are more sophisticated in their choice of leisure activity and the women in the partnership are having more say in where they go and what they do. Cultural classes such as studies in art and history as well as courses in aromatherapy are replacing the old golf and karaoke routine of the salary-men of long ago.

This trend reflects Japan's changing demographics, which shows an ageing population and a more feminine one too. This is occurring across the entire Japanese economy (and society as a whole), with more Japanese women shareholders, entrepreneurs and consumers than ever before playing an important role in the share market and even in foreign currency markets. Japanese women are numerically also having more influence politically. If you think Bill Clinton's 'soccer moms' were important in 1996, just wait until you see the economic and political influence of Japanese women in future years.

However, in order to further realise these gains, there is scope for more reform in the Japanese service sector, particularly in health, education and the lifestyle sector. According to Professor James Kondo of Tokyo University: 'The healthcare, education and the leisure sectors have traditionally been closed in Japan, but this will soon change to Australia's benefit. We still haven't realised the impact of the growth of Japan's mature-age cohort—and the spending power of mature-age Japanese women.'

So if the *shinkansen* ride was the highlight of Osaka Expo in 1970 over three and a half decades ago, what about Aichi Expo in 2005? There were two that stood out.

The first was legendary guitarist Tommy Emmanuel playing an amazing set at the Australian pavilion which even had the suits of the Japanese-Australian Joint Business Conference rocking. Seeing the heads of companies like Santos, Rio Tinto, BHP Billiton and Woodside jive away to 'our Tommy' was really something for both Aussie and Japanese observers alike (and good on them, too!).

The second was a robot impersonating a human being at the visitor information counter. The robot replicated a young, attractive Japanese woman dressed like a JAL flight attendant. She could answer all your questions in Japanese and English and in fact, so lifelike was she that many male visitors to the expo—maybe under the influence of too much Asahi beer—were propositioning her. Amazingly, the robot engineers had thought of everything, and any pick-up lines were met with an immediate response: 'Questions of a personal nature should be directed to my manager.' There's no way that kind of reply could be 'lost in translation'!

6 SWITCHED ON IN SEOUL

Aussie technology companies are making it bigger in South Korea than in any other market in the world. In fact, many use South Korea as a 'test-bed' for products that they haven't even sold in the Australian market yet. And quite a few Korean-Australians are playing a role in South Korea's digital revolution. Why is this so? The airport economist travels to 'switched-on' Seoul to find out.

PAUL LEE GREW up in Sydney. In Australia, after school, he worked in one of the many family businesses, including a duty-free shop in Castlereagh Street and as a tour guide, taking international visitors from Bondi to the Blue Mountains. Then in 1995, he was restless and decided he needed a sea change. But instead of heading up the coast to Byron Bay, or even a sleepier capital city, Paul swapped Sydney for the hustle and bustle of Seoul, the city of his birth. According to Paul, when I spoke to him in his studio in the hip part of Seoul, he tried everything on arriving in South Korea. 'We sold windsurfers, Aboriginal t-shirts, micro-irrigators for greenhouses (Koreans love greenhouses), even zinc cream!' he recalled. 'But it was tough. Learning to do business here is like learning another language.' However, despite some hit-and-miss early ventures, Paul seems to have found his niche selling designer jewellery to South Korea's highly fashion-conscious youth. And he came up with a novel way to sell his wares. 'Without an established brand name it was hard to break into the market, so I have used "star marketing" and it works like a charm,' he says. Paul engaged a number of key South Korean stars of song and screen, including 'South Korea's own Kylie Minogue', Lee Hyo Lee (better known as 'Finkl') and a number of top soap opera stars. He even engaged a well-known celebrity of the canine variety (wearing one of Paul's jewelled dog collars—for the Korean pet who has everything), but unfortunately the four-legged celebrity disgraced himself on the red carpet at the store opening in what turned out to be a dog-day afternoon. However, apart from this unfortunate incident, the star-marketing strategy has enabled Paul's company, Cocos & Co., to go from strength to strength on the back of the 'Bico' brand, buoyed also by Koreans' love of home-shopping channels.

But Paul is not the only Korean-Australian entrepreneur in the marketplace. For example, Jim Lim, another Sydney-sider, moved to Seoul in 1999 to head up Reach, a telecommunications company which is a joint venture between Telstra and Hong Kong telco PCCW-HKT. Jim describes himself as a '1.5' generation Korean-Australian rather than an outright first or second generation. Jim moved to South Korea when he realised he had lost touch with his friends from the Korean church community he grew up with in Sydney. 'None of them seemed to be around, then I realised they're all over here!'

Similarly, Min-Joo Sohn was born in South Korea but grew up in Perth and was educated at the University of Western Australia and the London School of Economics. Min-Joo is now an Australian Trade Commissioner in Seoul and helps Australian clients find their feet in South Korea. She says she sometimes feels 'a bit culturally schizophrenic' but that ultimately she 'belongs to both cultures'.

So, are the examples of Paul, Jim and Min-Joo unusual? According to Korean-born Australian biotechnology adviser Jo Kim, 'The 2001 Census says there were around 40,000 Koreans living in Sydney'. There is anecdotal evidence that some of them are starting to try their luck back in the land of their birth (or their parents' birth), although it would be fewer than the number of returnees heading back to China, India or parts of Europe. Given the strong connection between business and immigration, the Korean-Australian community could be a good means by which to build export and business links between the two countries. Jo Kim agrees: 'We are highlighting the importance of trade to the Korean-Australian community through local radio stations and newspapers.'

But is the 'return' of Korean-Australians (even 1.5 generation ones) a sign of South Korea opening up to the world and, particularly, to Australia? Bill Brummit, of the Australian Embassy in Seoul, says there are clear trends showing that the Korean economy is becoming increasingly open. 'Korea has basically gone from a hermit to a hub economy in a little over twenty years,' he explains. Why has this occurred? It's partly about trade and technology and partly about institutions. According to Brummit, trade and investment have played important roles in South Korea's success: 'Increased openness to trade and foreign direct investment has helped lift Korea's rate of economic development and the living standards of the South Korean people, and Australia has been a strong participant in Korea's progress.'

Dr Inseok Shin of the Korean Development Institute, a prestigious economic think-tank in Seoul, agrees. 'Our openness to trade and foreign direct investment helped Korea recover from the IMF crisis in 1997. Fortunately, Korea has a very strong IT sector and we could attract foreign capital when it was really needed,' he explains when I visit him at his office.

The technologically driven information age has also brought more democracy and openness to Korean society.

Former president Kim Dae-jung brought in social and democratic reforms in the 1990s, and his successor in the new
millennium, President Roh Moo-hyun, was a former human
rights lawyer. The down-to-earth President Roh was known as
Arjoshi, which means 'the neighbourly president' or 'the
people's president', as he had never been out of Korea
before his first official visit to Washington as head of state.
However, by his own admission, President Roh had some
difficulties adjusting to his new role and he was later
succeeded by Lee Myung-Bak from the Grand National Party,
who was a former Hyundai executive and Mayor of Seoul.

In fact, political reforms have also been accompanied by
structural reforms in Korean economy and society. According
to Dr Inseok Shin, there has been a decline in the influence
of the *chaebols* (Korea's large international corporations) and
an emergence of small-business-driven economic activity.
'The decline of the *chaebols* was a psychological blow to
Korea,' he says. 'Before 1997, we had not had one single
banking crisis in our history. But then Korea moved quickly to
remove indebtedness and we recovered quickly from the IMF
crisis.' On the decline of the *chaebols*, Jim Lim agrees: 'The
younger people, they just won't work for the *chaebols*, they are
more interested in working for smaller outfits or becoming
entrepreneurs themselves.' Structural reforms also have social
implications. Family sizes are becoming smaller, with higher
levels of disposable income. For instance, many Korean
couples with only one child are investing more in education,
even at preschool levels. This has led to some good opportunities for Australian companies like Melbourne-based
Gymbaroo, which has set up a joint venture with Kindyroo to
provide preschool activities using gym equipment featuring
Australian images.

So how have the changes in Korea affected the ability of
foreign companies—particularly Australian companies—to
do business in Korea? According to Elizabeth Masamune,
Australia's Senior Trade Commissioner in Seoul, the overall

picture is 'looking good, with Australian businesses covering a vast range of products and services in Korea'.

She adds that 'we are traditionally a commodity exporter, with petroleum, coal, beef, wool and iron ore featuring. In Korea you can also find Australian wine, cheese and oranges, but you can find racehorses, film production services, financial software and children's books as well'. Australians are also doing well in the export of automotive components and in knowledge-based services. 'Australia has had a number of key trade missions to Korea for education, biotechnology and IT,' Masamune comments. 'We are also planning a mission for financial services.' Australia and Korea are joining forces on several other key initiatives, for instance, the Korea Energy Economics Institute and Australian Bureau for Agricultural and Resource Economics recently finished major research on the export opportunities for liquefied natural gas in Korea after the success of this product in China.

But the most important thing about Korea is that it is a good place to try out new Australian technology and, if you are an IT exporter, then some of the wise heads in the industry say that you should go to Korea. 'They're all gadget crazy,' explains Elizabeth Masamune. 'South Korea is a great "test-bed" for IT products. Some Australian IT exporters even try Korea before testing out their product on the Australian consumer,' she explains.

Why is this so? As always, it all comes down to connections—broadband connections, that is. Indeed, in terms of international comparisons, Korea is consistently at the top of the heap. According to OECD data, at the time of the airport economist's first visit to Seoul, Korea had 12.2 million Internet subscribers (representing 25.4 per cent of the population), which is second only to Iceland on a per capita basis (26.7 per cent) and ahead of the Netherlands (25.3 per cent), Denmark (25 per cent) and Switzerland (23.1 per cent). On a per capita basis Korea also had greater broadband pen-

etration than its regional counterparts in East Asia, such as
Japan and Hong Kong, and the United States. Korea is also top
of the pops in terms of fibre-based broadband connections.

As Jim Lim explained to the airport economist, this is
partly because of the population density of South Korea.
'With 45 per cent of the population living in the Seoul/
Kyongi province in large apartment blocks, technologies like
broadband can spread quickly. That's why you have such
high Internet connections and mobile usage. The Internet is
in 79 per cent of all homes in Korea and mobile penetration
is around 63 per cent,' he says. So as far as trying out new
technology goes, as Jim says: 'If it works in Korea, there's a
fair chance that it will work in your home market.'

Elizabeth Masamune has taken advantage of this Seoul
situation and made South Korea a target market for
Australian IT. 'Korean customers are regular participants
in the major broadband summits in Australia and are
constantly receiving calls for Korean contacts from potential
Australian IT exporters,' she says. According to Masamune,
the Korean government is also preparing for the 'next wave'
of the information age by actively supporting and pro-
moting the implementation of infrastructure to make Korea
a global pioneer in terms of digital content. 'The rapid
adoption of new digital media broadcasting [as well as]
online and mobile technologies—including games, education and entertainment content—in Korea has created an
unprecedented demand for good quality content for these
emerging media channels,' she explains. To take advantage
of this new market opportunity, Austrade Seoul regularly
hosts digital content missions so that Australia's most innovative companies can strut their stuff for an eager Korean
audience.

Korea's transition from a war-torn, fractured, poor
economy to a mature, industrialised, sophisticated one
makes it one of the great economic development stories of
the past fifty years, but how did they do it?

First, the power of its IT connections, the so-called 'hermit to hub' phenomenon that Bill Brummit spoke about, has really helped Korea. The capacity to adopt sophisticated technologies quickly and add value in terms of innovation has hastened a societal transformation and raised Korea's profile and standing in the global economy.

Second, the institutions matter as well. Korea has been keen to work on its democracy and corporate governance since the Asian financial crisis. President Roh Moo-hyun survived a no-confidence motion early in his term and his government worked to further strengthen civil society and build up South Korea's social institutions . . . although the brawls in the parliament indicated that sometimes South Korean democracy is a little bit more 'robust' than it needs to be.

Third, South Korea has had to take advantage of the revival of inter-Asian trade and the growth in industrial production. More than any other economy in the region, South Korea has relied on growth in net exports for its recovery. Korea-watchers such as Duncan Wooldridge of UBS have been concerned about 'the ability of the consumer economy to sustain 4.5 to 5 per cent [growth] per year', but see construction and record exports as major drivers of Korean economic activity.

Of course, not everything in South Korea is modern and high-tech; tradition and hierarchy still abound to some degree. According to Elizabeth Masamune, 'In some parts of Korean society, they still have what they call "wife training school", with tips like "never tell a husband what to do, never wear noisy shoes"!' But many other sections of Korean society are open, cosmopolitan and interested in all things artistic. 'Korean pop culture is influential throughout Asia (it's known as *Hallyu* or the "Korean Wave"), the theatre scene is strong and its performing arts are as vibrant as ever. Accordingly, there's great scope for Australian creative exports as well in Korea,' Masamune says.

So there are export opportunities in South Korea whether you're high culture or high-tech. And as the opening up of the South Korean economy will attract many more Australian businesses to the market, maybe we'll see more Korean-Australians like Paul Lee, Jim Lim, Min-Joo Sohn and Jo Kim building the bridges between Sydney and Seoul.

7 MUMBAI BE RIGHT, I MAY BE CRAZY

Is watching Sachin Tendulkar bat on home soil in a Test match and meeting a famous Bollywood actress in one week as good as it gets? It could be, as the airport economist travels to India. Is India's relationship with Australia more than 'cricket, curry and Commonwealth'? And have Australian companies been able to climb aboard the rise of the world's next economic superpower?

MUMBAI (FORMERLY KNOWN as Bombay) is famous for its 'cricket gods' (like Tendulkar and Sunny Gavaskar) and Bollywood stars, but it is also the 'Gateway to India' and a thriving commercial and trading metropolis of over 19 million people. Indeed, Mumbai must be seen to be believed. A mass of poverty and desperation on the one hand but an amazing hub of entrepreneurship and dynamic capitalism on the other, Mumbai is full of contradictions. Mumbai was one of the key centres visited by a New South Wales trade mission to India organised by the Australia–India Business Council. The mission took in New Delhi, Mumbai and later Bangalore, covering a range of industries, from software, infrastructure and medical technology to higher education. Nearly 2000 Australian companies export to India, but there are many more opportunities to tap into.

But for a cricket tragic, Mumbai is fantastic. On the final day of a dramatic fourth Test, Mumbai's Wankhede Stadium was a full house of Indian cricket supporters cheering on their heroes. Outside the stadium, the lure of cricket is everywhere to be seen. On grounds next to Mumbai's High Court, the university and all across the city, thousands of cricket fanatics are playing matches, as they do every day all over the subcontinent. The airport economist, it should be said, was very fortunate that the then NSW premier Bob Carr, himself no sports fan, was leading the delegation, so some tickets were up for grabs. This is something that may not have happened had cricket fanatics like former prime ministers Bob Hawke or John Howard been in charge. Fortunately, all those I wanted to interview were also at the cricket, so it was only a matter of 'when in Rome . . .' (especially when you are in Mumbai).

Because of this important bilateral link between the two countries, Australian cricketers are themselves very visible exports to India. Fast bowler Brett Lee seemed to be on every billboard and Matthew Hayden's cooking tips popped up in almost every lifestyle magazine in Mumbai. Lee later recorded a song with a famous Bollywood singer to much acclaim. Driving the Mumbai streets, I was struck by a large advertising banner for the local beer, Kingfisher, which declared to all and sundry: 'One Indian the Aussies can't beat!'

But all this cricket talk is good news for Australia, opening up opportunities for our exporters everywhere. For example, in the cricket arena itself, Sydney company Albion is getting in on the act on the subcontinent. Albion, which manufactures the iconic Australian Test XI 'baggy green' cap and protective helmets, was in Mumbai for the fourth Test in order to meet some Indian distributors. According to Albion's General Manager, Ross Barrat, 'We see India as a major source of expansion for our product. We were founded in 1947—the same year as India's independence—and see our future wrapped up with India's just as we have a shared history.'

But it's not just cricket companies that are doing well in India; many other Australian organisations are leveraging the cricket relationship. Whilst in New Delhi, I visited the Indian office of the Snowy Mountains Engineering Corporation (SMEC). SMEC is involved in major infrastructure projects throughout South Asia and, as part of its community development initiative, sponsors young Indian cricketers. SMEC's Indian General Manager, David Tow, explains that 'whilst we are here in India to provide expertise in highways, irrigation and water resource management, we also want to help the community in other ways'.

Other Australian companies also have links to charitable foundations in India. For instance, Cochlear, the famous Australian inventor of hearing implants, has a joint venture with Indian-based Medilife Technologies, which provides clinics, medical training and other health facilities to patients in India. According to Brendan Murray, Cochlear's General Manager for the Asia-Pacific (Southern Area/Australasia), 'We are almost up to our 500th implant in India, which is very exciting for the company and for the health and well-being of the Indian community.' In fact, one of Cochlear's ear implants had been provided to a former Miss Universe (the airport economist was going to write an article with the headline 'Shock! Horror! Miss Universe has implants' but thought better of it).

And if too much cricket is finally enough in Mumbai, there's Bollywood too! Supran Sen, Secretary-General of the Film Producers Guild of India, gives me a rundown of the industry. 'There are nearly 1000 films made in India each year, the majority of which are made in Mumbai. The films are made to satisfy the 20 million plus patrons who visit the country's 13,000 cinemas every day. The films are made mainly in Hindi but translated into twenty-four languages,' he explains. India has always had a strong local film industry culture, although nowadays there has been a meshing of the traditional with the western. A brief viewing of Indian MTV gives you evidence of this where recent features such as *The Guru*, starring Heather Graham, show alongside *Bride and Prejudice*, starring Aishwarya Rai.

Bollywood's rise is also good news for Australia. Many Indian producers film commercials and movies in Australia because of our locations, the skill of our film crews—and the fact that the Bollywood stars won't get mobbed walking the streets of Australian cities as they do in Mumbai or Kolkata! According to Sen, 'Indian film producers like the legendary Feroz Khan love shooting in Australia. Australia has a good reputation here in Bollywood and we could do so much more together.'

However, despite its grip on the world's imagination, Mumbai to many people—both Indian and foreign—is not India. Neither, for that matter, is New Delhi, according to some. Just as the southern region of the United States is described as 'another country', when the airport economist ventured south he found a very different India. Whether it be the manufacturing hub of Chennai, the high-tech city of Bangalore, or the 'education state' of Kerala (famed for its near 100 per cent literacy levels), the south of India stands out for its economic dynamism and openness.

Chennai, the capital of the state of Tamil Nadu, is regarded by many as the commercial capital of southern India. Known as 'the Detroit of Asia' due to its automotive facilities, Chennai is also building a strong telecommunications presence thanks to Nokia (Finnair provides direct flights between the corporation's home town of Helsinki and Chennai), and it also has a busy port and related transport facilities in road and rail.

Known in colonial times as Madras (and Mumbai as Bombay, and Kolkata as Calcutta), the city was always called Chennai in the Tamil language and it is now its official name. Chennai is probably best known to many Australians as the place where Australian cricketer Dean Jones made 210 in the famous Madras tied test. Jones batted for almost two days with temperatures in the high 40s in an amazing act of endurance. Violently ill several times during his time at the crease, Jones was immediately taken to Chennai Hospital in a critical condition after that innings.

And despite the lingering perception that Australian exporters need Dean Jones-like endurance to do business in India, it seems there are plenty in southern India willing to give it a go. Just strolling through the Chennai city centre— one of India's new modern shopping malls, fuelled by the retail boom and a burgeoning young middle-class—gives you a flavour of the Australian presence. There the airport economist saw plenty of familiar brand names, such as Cookie Man and Florsheim shoes. In addition, legendary Australian basketballer Andrew Gaze has set up a franchise, Juz Sports, to sell basketball clothing and accessories in India (proving there's more to Australia–India relations than cricket). Just Cuts, Rip Curl, Billabong and Gloria Jeans are also planning to make their moves.

To handle the increased demand from Australian businesses in the south, Australia has opened up new offices in Chennai, with a handful of Australian states having a presence in both Bangalore and Chennai. Australia's Trade Commissioner in Chennai, Aminur Rahman, says this has been in response to the rise of Chennai and its economic importance to the south, and indeed to the rest of India's growing economy. 'Everything's hot in Southern India— including the temperature!' he jokes. 'Our patch extends from Chennai to Bangalore and even into Kerala. The diversity of the region is bringing in a wealth of opportunity: Chennai's strength in manufacturing is well-known but it is building up its high-tech capability, Bangalore is well-known as the home of computer icons Infosys and Wipro and aviation, whilst Kerala is strong in education and medical services.'

And speaking of southern exposure, the southern states of South Australia and Victoria have been particularly active in southern India. Many Adelaide automotive-component manufacturers (such as toolmakers like NTS, Trident and Precise) are joining the automotive global supply chain in Chennai. In addition, 70 per cent of the Ford Fiesta model assembled at the Ford plant in Chennai was designed by Ford Australia in Victoria. Further manufacturing opportunities are expected to come in food processing, a relatively unde-veloped opportunity in India for Australian companies, and in engineering and logistics.

South Australia has also been active in the areas of renew-able energy and climate change, thanks to the energetic premier, Mike Rann. The Tamil Nadu government's repre-sentatives have worked closely with their counterparts in Adelaide on Australia's export capabilities in solar power, wind power and other forms of environmental technology, with high-profile Indian corporation Tata setting up the Energy Research Institute in Chennai to support South Australia's Solar City initiative. This complements Australia's involvement in providing environmentally sustainable architecture and design expertise to the 2010 New Delhi Commonwealth Games project team.

It seems many international companies in India have got the message to 'go south' and, on current trends, Chennai (along with Bangalore and Kerala) will become more familiar to Australians than just being the scene of that famous tied test and marathon innings of one Dean Jones. So as Australia–India trade links start to widen and deepen, the relationship between the two will become more than the three C's—cricket, curry and Commonwealth—but Tendul-kar at Wankhede and Aishwarya Rai on a Bollywood movie set isn't a bad place to start.

THE MIDDLE EAST
AND AFRICA

8 SHEIKH, MODEL AND MALL

Dubai's skyline is rising, as are the fortunes of a lot of Australian expatriates trying their luck in the Middle East (tax-free, of course!). But is Dubai's prosperity just a mirage in the desert? The airport economist investigates.

AT FIRST GLANCE Dubai, a major global city in the United Arab Emirates (UAE) and the modern gateway to the Middle East, is on the up and *out*.

We may know about the skyscrapers and the cranes (many of them courtesy of Multiplex) dominating the skyline, but on my debut visit the airport economist found that Dubai is going in for expansion of a different kind, with new shopping malls, marinas and various lifestyle activities to entertain the occupants of all those high-rise apartments.

Under construction are Burj Dubai, Dubai Mall and Mall of Arabia in Dubailand, plus a series of offshore artificial island settlements such as The Palm Deira and The Palm Jebel Ali. So why all this focus on malls? 'It's basically because the locals like to shop, and it's too hot for the expatriates to do anything else with their kids in the middle of the day,' says Peter Linford, Australia's Dubai-based Senior Trade Commissioner for the Middle East.

Linford has seen a massive growth in Australian companies settling in Dubai to launch their Middle East operations. 'It's a real gateway to the region, like a Singapore or Hong Kong. And with Emirates having its hub here, it's a great place for Australian exporters to base themselves for doing business in the Gulf States, the Middle East in general and even North Africa, where new opportunities are beginning to be tapped into,' he adds.

Linford's observations are certainly backed up by the data. In the mid-2000s, almost as many Australian companies were exporting to the UAE as to the whole of India. This is probably due to the *entrepot* (trading hub) role that the UAE play for the region, with many imports to Dubai being re-exported to other markets in the Middle East.

The new developments in Dubai have certainly brought in many great opportunities for Australian companies, and the airport economist seemed to overhear Australian accents all over town when attending business functions.

Nowhere is that more apparent than at the still unfinished 'mother of all malls', Burj Dubai, where evidence of a 'kangaroo mafia' in the UAE is rife. At Burj Dubai, the leasing of the shops is managed by Melbourne's Jeanette Bennett and Fred Douglas, the architectural design is by Woods Bagot, the food concept for the mall is being undertaken by Future Foods (a small Melbourne niche exporter) and the mall's aquarium (containing 35,000 tropical fish and a good handful of sharks and stingrays) is being installed by Melbourne company Oceanis.

In fact, even before construction, the model for the entire site's master plan was made by Matthew Roche, who co-owns and manages the Sydney firm Modelcraft. After getting steady work in Australia for many years, Roche thought the only way to expand his company was to go global. A year and a half of flying in and out of Dubai later, he moved himself and his family to Dubai. According to Roche, 'Having an actual presence in the Middle East really helps to build your export business. Relationships really matter in Dubai; that's why we have to be here on the ground. There's no shortage of competition (mainly from the UK, Lebanon and the subcontinent) but we win projects through the quality of our work and the relationships we have built up locally.'

Demand is not a problem for leading Australian architecture firm Woods Bagot, either. The firm's lead partner in Dubai, Mark Mitcheson-Low, explains: 'We are not a remote outpost in Dubai. Our office does as much work as our London office. We can be choosy with the projects we do as there's plenty of work here.' Woods Bagot, like Modelcraft, has benefited from having a local presence in Dubai to service its clients in the Gulf States. 'In 1997, I used to fly-in fly-out from Perth, but I have been here since 2001 and it's made a big difference to client relationships and camaraderie amongst our architects in the office here,' says Mitcheson-Low. 'Woods Bagot's ambition is to be the signature architect to the world. We not only aim to be the best in the world technically, but we want every design to capture the culture of the region. Our designs in the UAE reflect the storytelling of the desert that has been there for thousands of years. That's what our clients want in a new building. My aim is to provide a story for every building through our unique designs,' he explains.

Local culture is important in Dubai, but there's also a strong demand for things international as well. According to Jeanette Bennett, Burj Dubai 'will cater to the strong demand for the world's leading consumer brands. We'll have the likes of Armani, as that's what both the local and global shoppers want'. Francis Loughran of Future Foods agrees. 'It's the same whether you are in Sydney, Melbourne or Dubai. The consumers want fresh sushi that tastes like sushi, and fresh juices that taste like it does everywhere,' he explains. However, Loughran warns other Australian companies venturing into the Middle East to be patient in terms of doing business. 'We had six meetings a day arranged for us during our first week here two years ago and we didn't hear anything for at least seven months. But once we heard it was on, it was all systems go—we've been flat out ever since. It's a case of when it rains, it really pours, which was ironic given that we're in the middle of a desert!' he says. 'We've been lucky, too, given that there are so many key Australians in all the right places in Dubai, from Emirates to Emaar Properties, and in all the hotels, hospitality and retail outlets.'

In fact, according to the Australian Consulate's James Wyndham, there are now around 15,000 Aussies here, compared to about 3000 six years or so ago. 'We form a reasonably large expatriate community along with Brits, the Irish, Bangladeshis, Indians, Pakistanis, Sri Lankans, South Africans and nationals of neighbouring Arab and North African states,' he says. 'There's plenty of English spoken in the UAE—you can hear the range of accents at the Dubai Rugby Sevens especially at Irish, South African, Welsh, Pacific Islander, Aussie and Kiwi games but also in offices and building sites around Dubai. However, the main advantage is that Australians are all in key strategic positions that are helpful to potential exporters to the Gulf States and the rest of the Middle East.'

In fact, Channel Nine's high-rating *Mornings with Kerri-Anne* is thinking of broadcasting some shows from Dubai, given the region's popularity with Australians. The Dubai Cup and the Rugby Sevens all get the Aussies over there, and host Kerri-Anne Kennerley herself has a special fondness for the region. 'Fashion and golf are two of my hobbies, and I am always astounded by the great energy and cultural diversity that awaits me on my regular visits there,' she says.

But with all this expansion, are there any problems awaiting the UAE? One side effect of Dubai's growth spurt is, of course, insufficient transport infrastructure. Dubai may have the population of Perth but it seems to have the traffic of Moscow, partially explained by the high-density living that comes with high-rise apartments as well as a lack of local public transport.

And speaking of high-rise apartments, does the building boom prick any concerns? According to the Victorian government's representative in Dubai, Peter Deacon, there are no signs yet of a bubble in Dubai's property market. Deacon, who has worked in the Middle East for over fifteen years, says: 'We are very conscious of property bubbles in Melbourne given Victoria's experience in the 1980s when we had lots of cranes on the skyline too, but Dubai does look to be in good shape. The asset base is strong and they are not investing with borrowed money.'

What of the future? It's a matter of living beyond oil. According to Peter Linford, 'There's plenty of diversification within the UAE, to Abu Dhabi and also elsewhere in the Gulf. This will bring new opportunities in education and training, environmental technology and agribusiness as well as in retail, hospitality, recreation and leisure activities.' Linford points to the example of the University of Wollongong's campus in Dubai and the success of leading agribusiness firms like GRM (led by the experienced Stewart Routledge) as great examples for others to follow.

Linford has also been instrumental in having the Australian Football League (AFL) host a pre-season game in Dubai. Given that Emirates sponsors Collingwood and Toyota sponsors the Adelaide Crows (Toyota's Australian division is a leading exporter to the Middle East), these teams were the obvious candidates for an AFL extravaganza in the desert. The AFL's Gillon McLachlan said in Melbourne that the 'Middle East is a prime region for our exhibition games after the success we've had in London, North America, South Africa and Asia.' And if the AFL is successful, we really will see the big men fly—all over the world, in years to come.

So expect bigger things for Australian companies in Dubai, the UAE and in the Gulf States and Middle East as a whole. Dubai will continue to be a place of growth and expansion with the UAE seeing beyond an energy-dependent economy. And look out for a lot more Aussie action at Burj Dubai. The mall is certainly in our court.

9 PROSPEROUS ON THE BOSPHORUS

Ankara is 'talking Turkey' to Brussels about joining the European Union. But is the land of Ataturk ready to become European? And will the Anzac football match suggested by some Turkish-Australian soccer fanatics take off in time for the big day?

SINCE HIS CLASSICAL studies days at high school, the airport economist has always wanted to visit Istanbul (or Constantinople, or Byzantium, as it was known in its previous incarnations). And with European Union (EU) accession on everyone's mind, it was a great time to visit this amazing city and the country of Turkey.

After the expansion of the EU into the former eastern bloc, all eyes naturally turned to the secular Islamic nation founded by Mustafa Kemal Ataturk. Whilst the EU accession talks, on recent form, tend towards a marathon rather than a sprint, Turkey's recent modernisation has certainly boosted the economic credentials it requires to join the European club: things have to be reasonably 'prosperous on the Bosphorus' for Turkey to get a guernsey in Brussels. But there's plenty of water to go under the many bridges (and mosques) that adorn this classically beautiful city.

So how is Turkey faring? Economically, it's a case of so far, so good. According to the Economist Intelligence Unit,

Turkey's economic growth prospects are robust, with annual rates of growth expected to sit at healthy levels. In fact, in terms of industrial components, Turkey's growth is faster than China's, and resource-rich Russia and Turkey are the sprinters of the emerging economies. Ironically, Turkey's growth rate currently outstrips the major economies in the very club it is trying to join.

Tevfik Aksoy, Deutsche Bank's Chief Economist for Turkey, was pleased with Turkey's economic performance when the airport economist met him in Istanbul. 'I would say that Turkey's economy is in its best shape in forty years. We have experienced strong levels of economic growth, low inflation and reasonable fiscal discipline in the past few years. The current government is reform-minded and is committed to raising productivity levels and undertaking essential privatisation programmes,' he explained.

Of course, this is a far cry from Turkey's recent economic history. 'When inflation was 60 per cent, we used to regard this as zero,' quips Gunduz Findikcioglu, Chief Economist of Turkiye Sinai Kalkinma Bankasi (TSKB, the Turkish equivalent of the old Commonwealth Development Bank in Australia). 'When I was at the World Bank, the Turkish economy was in [one of] two states—either in crisis or in a mini-crisis. Things got particularly bad during the 1994 crisis when the value of the exchange rate tripled in three months,' he explains. However, Dr Findikcioglu now regards the Turkish economy as being 'in reasonable shape', with government debt at around only 3.3 per cent of GDP, 'well below Maastricht Treaty levels' (as prescribed by the EU when admitting new members), and fewer bankruptcies in the financial private sector. 'The TSKB has not had a non-performing loan in the past five years,' he adds.

So what are Turkey's trade prospects? Of course, Istanbul (especially when it was Constantinople and Byzantium) has always been a trading hub, acting as a bridge between Europe, Asia and the Middle East. Its trade in modern times

is based heavily around the neighbourhood, as Ahmet
Ereclin, HSBC's General Manager for Turkey, points out.
'Turkey is in an excellent geographical position trade-wise.
When things are slow in Western Europe, we can look north
to Russia, or east to Central Asia. Alternatively, we can go
south to the Middle East and North Africa, where we have
strong cultural and trading ties.' Ereclin says Turkey's manufacturing sector (especially in textiles and motor vehicles) is,
'like everybody', concerned about the rise of China,
although increased international competition from the Far
East 'will be beneficial for raising innovation and productivity in the local manufacturing sectors'.

However, it can't all be good news in Turkey, particularly
with constitutional issues to sort out in the lead-up to the
EU accession. And whilst the economic outlook for Turkey
is solid, there are some risks concerning fiscal discipline,
currency volatility and geopolitical issues locally. Tevfik Aksoy
of Deutsche Bank believes the main economic risks are the
current account deficit (which is around 6.2 per cent of
GDP) and Turkey's vulnerability to exchange rate volatility
and mood swings in the capital market, or 'hot money'. He
also thinks that how the government handles the sensitive
issues of Cyprus and human rights will be critically important. 'Of course, EU accession matters, and it will take
between ten and fifteen years. However, the reforms required
to join the EU are essential for Turkey's economic future in
any case. Reforms that help raise productivity, upgrade our
infrastructure and ease our fiscal burdens will help
modernise Turkey's economy,' he says.

Whilst the issue of EU accession dominates the headlines,
market analysts have to some extent factored in the point
that the negotiations between Ankara and Brussels are now
'qualified', reducing the economic risks associated with a
protracted accession process. Fortunately, many Turkish
commentators are patient and have a strong belief in their
political institutions. As Ahmet Ereclin remarks, 'Don't

forget, Turkey has been a secular Islamic democracy for seventy-five years, with a strong commitment to free markets. This is a pretty unique position to be in. So why worry about another ten years?'

So what does Turkey's economic resurgence mean for Australia? Research by Austrade reveals that there are almost 300 Australian exporters who do business with Turkey, which makes it a medium-range market. Australia has a strong presence in oil and gas, infrastructure, information and communication technologies (ICT), and food and beverage, with a growing presence in service areas such as education, healthcare and recreation. Some examples include Austal, whose fast ferries ply Istanbul's waters; Ottoman Petroleum and Incremental Petroleum, both large foreign investors in Turkey; and Oceanis, a Melbourne-based builder of aquariums (which has had great success in Shanghai, Pusan and Bangkok and is now looking to Paris, Prague, Copenhagen and Dubai as well as Istanbul).

One thing driving opportunity in Turkey is the 'Young Turk' factor, and with 50 per cent of the Turkish population under twenty-five, this also helps Australia's prospects, particularly Australian education providers but also Australian SMEs looking to broaden their customer base. Turkey's young population also has important implications for EU accession. As HSBC economist Esra Erisir explains, 'Old Europe is literally old, with an ageing population and a pension programme that needs funding. Turkey has lots of young people who need work. That's why so many move westwards.' Indeed, there are many young Turks working in Europe—according to Erisir, 2.5 million in Germany alone. This did not gone unnoticed by former Australian Trade Commissioner in Instanbul Damien Fisher, a German speaker who regularly organised Turkish elements to Australian–German trade missions. 'With such a strong Turkish-German trade link, it is important to take advantage of these networks to see if there is any benefit to Australian business potentially at play,' he says. His recent successor Geoff Rea has continued those missions and has also forged ahead in new sectors. 'Further opportunities exist in technical education, agribusiness and environmental technologies all over Turkey,' Rea says.

However, there is another important element to exploit in Australian-Turkish relations—our mutual history forged at Gallipoli. Every year on Anzac Day hordes of Australians travel to Gallipoli to pay their respects to fallen forebears. The Australian, New Zealand and Turkish governments have taken great effort to make the peninsula, now a national park, an effective monument to their memory.

Many Turkish-Australians have also been keen to highlight the importance of Anzac Day, one idea being to take advantage of the community ties that sport provides. During the lead-up to the 2006 FIFA World Cup, at the well-respected Lowy Institute for International Policy, the airport economist spoke at a 'Football Diplomacy' conference about the links between geopolitics, economics, trade and football (soccer). No doubt buoyed by the success of the Australian national football team—affectionately known as 'the Socceroos'—in making the FIFA World Cup finals, the speakers at the Lowy Institute were waxing lyrical about the political and diplomatic implications of football. Amidst some of the 'big picture' presentations came a practical suggestion from Tarkan Batgun, a leader of the Sydney Turkish community. Tarkan suggested that it was time to commemorate the Anzac-Turkish relationship with an annual football event between Australia, New Zealand and Turkey. 'Given how important Gallipoli is to Australia and New Zealand, and given how important the Canakkale Wars are to Turkey, and given that we are all mad on sport, why not play soccer on or around Anzac Day each year?' he asked.

In fact, Tarkan has already started the ball rolling with a Gallipoli Tri-Nations football tournament and is doing his bit to get the idea accepted in Ankara and with the Turkish community in Australia. The airport economist hooked up with Tarkan and some of his Turkish-Australian colleagues in Istanbul and noticed his footprint all over Istanbul and Ankara as well as in the Turkish communities of Sydney and Melbourne. And the great champion of Australian football, SBS commentator Les Murray, another brilliant Hungarian (see chapter 13), has been enlisted to help the Gallipoli tri-Nations football cause. After all, Tarkan does have a point. We have many sporting rivalries with other nations—the Ashes against England in cricket, the Bledisloe Cup against New Zealand in rugby union—so why not one with Turkey? Being something of an entrepreneur, Tarkan is using his membership of the Galatasaray football club (the Turkish equivalent of Liverpool or Real Madrid) to build up links with Turkish expatriate communities worldwide.

Whilst it is important to keep Anzac Day and the memories of fallen soldiers clear of other events—sporting or otherwise—on 25 April, Tarkan's idea of forging closer ties between Australia and Turkey through sport is a noble gesture. After all, Turkey has done much to help Australia and New Zealand commemorate this day of the year that is so important to our history. The most moving event of the airport economist's life was visiting Anzac Cove and imagining what it was like for those young men who landed on the beaches under fire, with minimal chance of survival. And the Turkish people have taken the Anzac story to their hearts as well. There is an inscription at Anzac Cove from a speech by war hero and modern Turkey's founder Ataturk:

> Those heroes that shed their blood and lost their lives . . .
> You are now lying in the soil of a friendly country. Therefore
> rest in peace. There is no difference between the Johnnies
> and the Mehmets to us where they lie side by side now here
> in this country of ours . . . you, the mothers, who sent their
> sons from faraway countries wipe away your tears; your sons

are now lying in our bosom and are in peace. After having lost their lives on this land. They have become our sons as well.

So the big picture is that Turkey may be knocking on Brussels' door, but there is still plenty of housekeeping to do back home. This modernisation process will drive forward ample business opportunities in Turkey, with a role for Australian companies and a chance to further strengthen and broaden the links forged in the aftermath of Gallipoli. Our shared history and the possibility of stronger commercial and sporting ties—especially in football—will perhaps help Australia and Turkey to also tread our future paths together.

10 TIM TAMS TO TEL AVIV

A former 'kibbutznik' himself, the airport economist investigates Australia's unusual trade ties with the Jewish state.

DID YOU KNOW that Tim Tams are kosher? It's true! And believe or not, the Aussie icon chocolate biscuit is one of Australia's newest exports to Israel.

According to Guy Elan of import–export company Guild Enterprises, about 700,000 packets of Tim Tams have been sold in Israel in each of the past four years at fifteen shekels (A\$4.70) a pop. 'We ship them straight from the Arnotts' factory in Sydney,' he says, adding that 'many young Israelis come to Australia after finishing their national service to study or relax, and they have developed a taste for the Tim Tam and spread the word back in Israel'.

Initially Guild Enterprises was only able to sell Tim Tams in non-kosher retail outlets, but Elan worked closely with Rabbi Moshe Gutnick in Sydney to get them into kosher supermarkets and department stores. According to Elan, this was a major breakthrough: 'Non-kosher outlets only accounted for 15 per cent of Israel's market. But now that Tim Tams are kosher we have been able expand our brand all over the country. And with Israelis being such perfectionists, there's also instructions in Hebrew on how to eat them the Australian way—we call it the Tim Tam suck!'

The Israeli tendency to strive for perfection was first noticed when the airport economist lived there in 1989, a time when relations between the Jewish state and its neighbours were pretty good (by Middle Eastern standards). The treaty with Egypt having been in place for a decade (with the Sinai desert handed back to Egypt), Israeli tourists were in fact visiting the Pyramids and sailing the Nile, and even relations with Jordan were quite settled. The intifada (Palestinian uprising) had not yet started to hit full swing, and even relations with Lebanon were improving.

The airport economist had come to Israel to write a paper for graduate school on the economics of the kibbutz, the distinctive Israeli collective society usually based around agriculture. In Israel's early years, many of the Ashkenazi Jewish migrants from Europe had grown up in households with leftist political leanings. As a result, many were active in intellectual and political circles such as the 'Bundist' trade union movement, based on Jewish teachings and traditions. In fact, many trade union leaders in the United States, Canada, Australia and Europe were also of Jewish origin, particularly in the early twentieth century. In the new state of Israel after the horror of the Holocaust, many European Jewish refugees wanted to set up a new society along collective principles and formed the kibbutz movement (which also had some antecedents amongst late nineteenth century Jewish immigrants to the region).

The kibbutzim were not only influential in Israel's early economic history, they were also important in Israel's successful efforts to irrigate dry land for farming and other innovative breakthroughs in Israeli agriculture. However, forty years on, when the airport economist himself became a kibbutznik, the kibbutz movement was on the wane and the kibbutz sector only accounted for 3 per cent of the Israeli economy. Somehow the collectivist spirit didn't last, although there were pockets of economic success for some kibbutzim.

For example, my kibbutz, Ramat Yochanan (in a small village close to Haifa), ran a very successful plastics business, Palram, which exported all over the world. The success of Palram enabled the kibbutz to diversify away from agriculture, although the airport economist found picking mangoes and avocados in the fields with thirty or so Israeli, American, Dutch and German women in their mid-twenties somehow provided more job satisfaction than working in the heat of the plastics factory. Besides, my grandfather, Kopel Harkowitz (a trainee rabbi, who changed his name to Ken Harcourt so he could become a Bondi lifesaver—or, in his owns words, go 'from the Goldbergs to the Icebergs')— had been a leather merchant and his industry usurped by the introduction of plastics, so I decided to object on philosophical grounds!

In fact, the airport economist's employment status on the kibbutz was not without controversy. Volunteering to be 'the kibbutz rabbi' (you know, go around, bless a few mangoes, say a few prayers) didn't go down too well either, especially given that the kibbutz was largely agnostic. But it was the airport economist's long-term plans that annoyed the old-timers on the kibbutz, given that I was writing a paper for the graduate school which I was to attend in the United States later that year. 'What do we need another economist for?' asked kibbutz elder statesman David Weiss, one of the many Holocaust survivors on our kibbutz. 'What good is an economist, or a philosopher, or a lawyer, when you need a plumber on the weekend? You should do a trade, learn to do something with your hands, something useful.'

The 'too much college, not enough knowledge' sentiments of David Weiss were widely held throughout the kibbutz. After all, there has been no shortage of intellectuals in Israel, and the continuing emigration of Jews from the Soviet Union to Israel was thought to be increasing the oversupply of highly educated people in the country. However, the development of a knowledge-based economy with a world-class IT and education infrastructure (along with well-developed venture capital) since the fall of communism in 1989 may show that the influx of highly educated workers has helped rather than hindered the Israel economy. Although Weiss's point about having a ready supply of plumbers and electricians does have validity—he just was talking to the wrong guy.

So how has Australia fared in the economic story of Israel? Of course, Australia has always had strong historical ties with Israel. When the Jewish state was established in 1948, the announcement to the General Assembly of the newly created United Nations (UN) was made in a broad Australian accent. That accent belonged to Dr H.V. Evatt, who was president of the UN as well as Australia's minister for external affairs. Along with providing political support to the newly created nation, Australia was influential in helping Israel develop economically by strengthening its trading ties to the rest of the world in the 1950s and 60s. After all, post-birth, Israel—unlike most countries—couldn't trade with its neighbours. It was also established at a time when world trade was adversely affected by protectionism as the General Agreement on Tariffs and Trade, the forerunner to the World Trade Organization, was also founded in 1948. In the face of these restrictions, Israel relied on immigration to build its economic links with the rest of the world and began forging ties with the USA, the UK, Canada, South Africa and Australia. As a result, Australia took a large proportion of imports from Israel in its early years in order to assist the fledgling state and has run (relatively small) trade deficits with Israel ever since.

How has Australia connected with Israel in more recent times? The airport economist met with Australia's Trade Commissioner to Tel Aviv, Eric Goldberg. 'Australia sells a range of products to Israel, from education to kosher food and wine, and a range of knowledge-based exports like biotechnology and medical technologies and related services,' he says. 'Israel's a small country, but there's always plenty of innovation and opportunities for investment, and Australia is always very well regarded here.'

In manufacturing, Australia also exports significant amounts of machinery and components to Israel. The aircraft industry has become a key knowledge-based exporter for Australia in Israel and Queensland-based Aeropower Pty Ltd, for example, is an electrical contractor that uses helicopters to wash electricity transmission insulators. The company's technology suits Israel's dry climate, which is similar to some of the outback regions of Australia.

But it is not just a matter of trade volumes and values. The quality of the trading relationship matters too, as does knowledge of the market and networks. For instance, Israel is an important source of knowledge transfer for Australia as it has been very successful at commercially exploiting its knowledge capital through strong links between education institutions and innovative enterprises. Israel, like the United States, has been able to commercially exploit the creative and scientific discoveries of its many graduates and has well-developed biotechnology, IT and venture capital sectors. So the old kibbutz saying 'too much college, not enough knowledge' doesn't hold in Israel, according to the recent evidence.

Israel has also successfully encouraged its graduates to establish global companies through venture capital and private business 'incubator' programmes, promoted by the Israeli Ministry of Industry, Trade and Labor with the Office of the Chief Scientist playing an instrumental role. By necessity, Israel has traditionally had to rely on exports and immigration, but the knowledge economy has enabled its high-technology industries to prosper as well.

People networks are just as important. For instance, many Australian entrepreneurs who came out of war-torn Europe have strong links to Israel. In fact, much of Australia's success as an exporting nation in the late twentieth century was due to the efforts of the postwar immigrants who ended up leading successful companies, with names like Abeles, Lowy and Pratt coming to mind. Many of these future business leaders came to Australia with no assets (and often no English) but with a range of contacts in their home markets, market experience and corporate savvy.

People networks are also clear in terms of the number of Australian exporters with links to Israel. Despite being a small economy, research by Austrade shows that Israel was our third highest trade partner in the Middle East region after oil-rich giants the United Arab Emirates and Saudi Arabia. The importance of Israel in terms of exporter numbers is in part due to the active role in developing business ties played by the Australia–Israel Chamber of Commerce (AICC), regarded by many international and local business professionals to be the best chamber of commerce in Australia. As AICC Chief Executive Anthony Hollis puts it, 'Trade and business is all about networking, whether between organisations within Australia, or on a bi-lateral basis. When it comes to international business, it all comes down to the schmoozing. And you have to be good, because in business, Israelis are perfectionists.'

There you go, it's that perfection thing again! Whilst on the kibbutz, I heard a joke about an Israeli couple making love in the street: 'How many people does it take to make love in the street in Israel? Two, but with ten others watching and giving advice on how to do it better!'

So, the lesson is that from love-making to Tim Tams, Israelis are certainly perfectionists, so you have to be on your toes in a sophisticated market like Israel.

11 FREE (TRADE) NELSON MANDELA

Many of us used to sing 'Free Nelson Mandela' in the apartheid years, but what is now happening in the 'new' South Africa? Is Australia involved in reviving the world's poorest continent?

THE AIRPORT ECONOMIST'S first visit to South Africa was in March 1995. Only eleven months after the momentous election of President Nelson Mandela, it was an exciting time to be in South Africa. I was sent by the Australian Council of Trade Unions to work with the African National Congress (ANC) and the Congress of South African Trade Unions (COSATU) on prices and incomes policies and, having previously met a number of key ANC officials in Australia, it was exciting to see them get the chance to put their policy ideas into practice in government.

On arrival in Johannesburg I was asked to present a paper on incomes policy to COSATU's research arm and then to the national executive. As in Australia, I put on a suit and tie and (rather foolishly, as it turned out) walked through downtown Johannesburg to the COSATU office in Leyds Street. Whenever my wife Jo and I stopped to ask directions, most locals said 'you drive here, then turn left' and so on. When we replied that we didn't have a car, there were shocked looks and the suggestion that we should both be certified. We received a slightly different response at the 'Wits' campus (the University of Witwatersrand) when we were given suspicious answers to every question, such as the following exchange:

'Excuse me, do you have the time?'

'Yes.'

'Well, can you tell me what it is?'

'What do you want to know the time for?'

Or this one:

'Excuse me, do you know the way to the bookstore?'

'Yes.'

'Well, can you tell me how to get there?'

'Why do you want to go to the bookstore?'

(Jo, in a state of disbelief:) '*Perhaps* to buy some books!'

Of course, when we got there, the university bookstore had one book in it, and was locked and burnt out due to a bombing the week before, which may have explained the exchange with the South African student. It may also be that years of living under apartheid had made suspicion the norm.

Once we got to COSATU headquarters and I set up for the seminar, the receptionist asked if I would like a cup of coffee.

'How do you take it?'

'Er—with milk?' I replied, wondering if it was bad form to say 'white'.

'It's okay—it's not a test,' she laughed, which helped lighten the mood. It didn't last, however. Just as I started my seminar paper on the Australian and South African economies, I was castigated by the researchers (who were predominantly white and sporting tie-dye shirts and pony-tails) for 'dressing like a boss'. I replied that in Australia, union officials often wore suits and that I would too if I was meeting a big South African company, so surely COSATU deserved the same respect. Fortunately, when I addressed the COSATU national executive that afternoon, who were predominantly black, they all turned out in—you guessed it—three-piece suits. I was sure glad I didn't take a walk back to the hotel to put on a tie-dye t-shirt and jeans!

As it happened, my 1995 visit coincided with the first official Australian trade delegation to South Africa since the end of apartheid, attempting to revive trade and investment between Australia and the new South Africa after the long years of economic isolation. This was followed by a number of exchanges of knowledge and information on a range of topics including pension policy (superannuation), education and training, public utilities and industrial relations. The 1995 trip also occurred in the year that sporting links were restored and South Africa hosted and won the Rugby World Cup, with the memorable sight of Nelson Mandela in a Springboks jersey raising the Webb Ellis Trophy (something that would have been considered unthinkable just six years earlier).

Even before the turbulent apartheid years there had been a great deal of historical interest in South Africa from an Australian point of view (and indeed much South African interest in Australia, too). There are a few reasons for this.

First, both countries have similarities in settlement patterns from Europe and a legacy of British institutions (with the addition of African, Dutch and Afrikaner influences in South Africa) and, even today, both are members of the Commonwealth. Second, there are strong people links. As immigrant societies, many South Africans and Australians share family ties and South Africans are becoming an influential immigrant group in Australia. Third, Australia and South Africa are both small, open economies, geographically isolated from major world markets with large, export-orientated resource sectors. And, of course, a strong Australian presence in the anti-apartheid struggle has made a difference, particularly since the new South Africa has begun rebuilding its economic and political institutions.

Both countries have also embraced economic reforms and share a commitment to openness in trade and invest-

ment and the need for social protection to achieve community support for such a course. In fact, many of the new
South Africa's own reforms have drawn on the Australian
experience. With the election of Nelson Mandela in 1994,
the new government introduced the Reconstruction and
Development Programme (RDP), outlining proposals for
jobs, housing, healthcare and social amenities for all. The
RDP was introduced together with related reforms in education and training, social protection, the promotion of small-
and medium-sized enterprises and the development of black
entrepreneurship. In terms of macroeconomic policy, the
Growth, Employment and Redistribution plan (GEAR) was
developed along with proposals for Reserve Bank independence. In trade policy, South Africa joined the newly
established World Trade Organization and opted for
openness in terms of trade and foreign direct investment.

On the airport economist's return visit to South Africa
more than a decade after the end of apartheid, the economic
and political landscape is a mixed bag. Many ANC activists and
trade unionists have joined the leadership ranks of business
and government; for instance, Cyril Ramaphosa became a
leading businessman after years of fronting the National
Union of Mineworkers during the anti-apartheid struggle, and
Tito Mboweni, the Minister of Labour, later became Governor
of the Reserve Bank of South Africa. However, change has not
only happened at the top but across all parts of South African
society. For example, in Soweto the Institute for Advanced
Journalism, set up by famous South African journalist and
political activist Alistair Sparks, is training young Sowetans to
become journalists. The programme has received assistance
from AusAID and the Australian trade union movement's aid
arm, APHEDA. At the forefront of this training is Australian
journalist Geof Parry, clearly an inspirational teacher to his
young troops from the townships.

Another change is of a more regional nature, with the
focus now moving towards 'the Cape' area rather than solely

on Johannesburg. Whilst in the small wine town of Stellenbosch near Cape Town, I gave a paper at its university. This
institution has a unique place in the history of South Africa,
being instrumental in both the formation and dismantling of
apartheid. In fact, the secret Afrikaner society the Broder-
bund (or brotherhood) was formed at the University of
Stellenbosch, and this society later created many of the institutions of apartheid. However, later on, the (mainly
Afrikaner) student body at the university was the first to rebel
against racialist policies. On my visit to the campus, I spoke
with many students who had characterised the multi-racial
classrooms in the new South Africa. Many are amazed at the
attitudes of the older apartheid era generation but are
cautiously optimistic about the country's future. Crime rates
are still a concern although there has been less capital flight
than had been expected. It puts into some perspective the
often used (and slightly cynical) saying: 'Who is a patriotic
South African? The bloke who can't sell his house.' If these
students are making an effort, surely the rest of the world can
give the new South Africa a break in moving on from its past?

So how has South Africa fared economically since
apartheid ended? On the international trade and investment
front, some comparative exporter surveys show South Africa
is ahead of the pack. For instance, in terms of exporter
expectations, export propensity and manufacturing employment driven by exports, South Africa is a world leader. For an
economy that was cut off from the world for so long, this is a
significant achievement.

Compared to Australia, South Africa has a different
export structure. Whilst both are significant resource
exporters, South Africa has a higher proportion of exports in
manufactures but is relatively underdeveloped in services.
And in terms of export destinations, South Africa is more
European-focused whilst Australia is relatively more Asian-
focused; the UK, Germany and Italy make up almost a third
of all South African exports, whilst Japan, China and Korea

are major destinations for Australian exports. The foreign investor brands in South Africa are mainly Dutch, German and British, with only a smattering of Japanese or Korean influence. (Under apartheid, Japanese businesspeople were made 'honorary whites' by the government so they could play golf and get around the country's business and government elite unimpeded.)

And what of Australian businesses' involvement in South Africa? After playing a leading role in the anti-apartheid movement, have Australians lost interest? There's certainly been activity in the mining and infrastructure sectors. Major Australian investors in South African mining include giants BHP Billiton and Western Australian consultancy company RSG Global. Macquarie Africa is also involved in major infrastructure projects following its success in Asia and the Middle East, and Monash University has a campus in the Johannesburg area. TAFE Global has also been active in increasing South Africa's investment in human capital through education and training. In fact, South Africa is easily Australia's most important market in Africa for trade and investment, so there's still strong Australian involvement in the post-apartheid era.

South Africa has come a long way under trying conditions since 1994. The South African government has to balance the expectations of its long-suffering citizens with the need for trade, investment and macroeconomic stability. However, like Australia, South Africa would benefit from more openness and fairness in the world trading system so that the work it has done at home—especially in terms of economic and social infrastructure—can be rewarded appropriately on the international stage. South Africa may have been closed to the world under apartheid, but the world should not remain closed to South Africa—and indeed the rest of Africa—in terms of trade. Let's hope there are brighter times ahead for the Rainbow Nation.

EUROPE

12 PUSHKIN MEETS PITJANTJATJARA

Why does Aboriginal art sell better when twinned with cosmetics in Moscow? And what is a Port Adelaide blanket salesman doing in St Petersburg in the middle of summer? The airport economist goes back to the former USSR and finds that, after a decade of turbulence, the Russian bear is turning bullish for Australian exporters.

OLIGARCHS, MAFIA AND terrorism in Chechnya are all images that come to mind when we think about Russia. However, the airport economist's first visit to Moscow and St Petersburg is a real eye-opener. The economy is improving, the financial system has stabilised and Russians are more accepting of the market system.

What is driving all this change?

First of all, Moscow's growth has been really dominating the new Russia commercially as well as politically, and it is now a real boomtown full of luxury cars, entrepreneurs on the make and large doses of conspicuous consumption. Surveys undertaken on the cost of living (often taken to determine the living-away-from-home allowances of expatriate businesspeople and trade commissioners) regularly rate Moscow as one of the world's most expensive cities, along with the likes of Tokyo and London. (In fact, Russians have also added their bit to London's escalating prices, especially when Russian businessmen buy football clubs like Chelsea.)

Second, the Russian oil and gas sector has been going from strength to strength and is attracting substantial foreign investment. For instance, Australia is playing a key role in Pacific Russia with the development of oil and liquefied natural gas on Sakhalin Island. When the airport economist interviewed Australia's Senior Trade Commissioner in Moscow, Gregory Klumov, Sakhalin was considered to be 'bigger than Ben Hur' for Australia–Russia trade relations. 'After all, over the life of the project it is estimated that US$100 billion will be invested. Big players like Shell, Exxon Mobil and BP are all involved,' he explains. According to Klumov, Australia is getting a major slice of the Sakhalin action with opportunities in 'infrastructure development, construction and engineering, catering, business and language training, transport, logistics and telecommunications'. There's plenty of action on Russia's Pacific coast for Aussie exporters, particularly when Sakhalin is quicker to get to from Sydney, albeit via Seoul, than it is from Moscow.

Third, after the roller-coaster ride of former leader Boris Yeltsin, President Vladimir Putin was keen for Russia to be a stable and influential force in the world. For instance, pursuit of World Trade Organization membership has been important to Putin as Russia engages in the world economy and becomes an important geopolitical player. Of course, the accession of many former eastern bloc states (such as Poland, the Czech Republic, Estonia, Latvia and Lithuania) to the European Union has not gone unnoticed by the Kremlin, who still understand the pride of the Russian populous. According to Klumov's recent successor, Dan Tebbutt, 'Russia is a proud nation, and is very conscious of its place in the world.'

As a result, for most of this decade Russia has been enjoying an economic resurgence. According to the Senior Economist of Nikoil (one of corporate Russia's energy giants), Vladimir Tikhomirov, GDP growth is expected to grow by between 5 and 7 per cent per annum over the next four years. 'Energy is a key strategic asset for Russia in the global economy, and high oil prices will help drive Russian economic performance, which has been sound since the 1998 financial crisis,' he explains to the airport economist in his Moscow office.

However, there is some caution in the Nikoil analysis. Tikhomirov, who taught at Melbourne University in the early 1990s, is conscious of Russia's over-reliance on commodities. During his stay in Australia, Tikhomirov was influenced by the seminal work of Australian economist Professor Bob Gregory on 'Dutch disease', which focuses on the exchange-rate effects of export sectors (such as agriculture and mining) on import-competing sectors (services and manufacturing). He has some concern about a similar effect occurring in Russia. 'Throughout the last century, Russia's economic curse lay in its heavy dependence on commodity exports, and we don't want to repeat that episode as we move towards a market economy in the twenty-first century,' he warns.

So how is Australia benefiting from Russia's new economic growth? According to Gregory Klumov, it is a matter of being better late than never. 'It is only in the late 1990s that large Australian companies began to take advantage of the Russian energy bonanza. The US, Germans and the Dutch have been here for a while. However, our strengths will really show—particularly in Pacific Russia,' he says.

Klumov's words proved prophetic in 2007 when then Russian President Putin led a two hundred-strong Russian business delegation to Australia to attend APEC. During the APEC meetings deals between Australia and Russian were signed in the fields of energy, mining-related services and financial services. The visit by Putin was the first ever to Australia by a Russian head of state.

But what lies beyond the energy sector, which is dominated by larger companies like Rio Tinto and BHP Billiton?

How are smaller Australian companies doing in the Russian market? Of course, some small players have been part of the energy boom too. Mining-related services and software have huge export potential in Russia. For example, Surpac Minex, a small Perth company that specialises in geological software, is now venturing into Russia after great success in India and China. According to CEO Andrew Pyne, the company is looking to open a representative office in Moscow and another in either Vladivostok or in Siberia. 'We've done well in India and China, with some good assistance from Austrade in those markets, but we really think Russia is the new frontier for the development of our business,' he says during our interview in Moscow.

But there are also many Australian entrepreneurs outside the energy sector taking the opportunity to set up in Russia. For example, Andrey Vakulin, a Port Adelaide-based entrepreneur, sells sheepskins, textiles, meat, wine and fertilisers to the Russian market. Andrey and his wife set up a family business after immigrating to South Australia from Russia in 1994, and they now have offices in Moscow and St Petersburg, with their global headquarters in Port Adelaide. Vakulin's East German-born European manager, Holger Albrecht, talks to me about the excitement of being an entrepreneur after many years of 'being told what to do' under communism in the old eastern bloc. Albrecht thinks that 'Australians are natural entrepreneurs as well as being friendly people' but 'that the market in Australia is just too small and there is never enough money to back the brilliant ideas that every Australian has, hence our expansion into Russia and Eastern Europe'.

A St Petersburg–focused entrepreneur, Russian-Australian Sergey Cherny thinks Australia has not seen the full potential of the Russian market. Cherny, who imports blankets and other woollen textiles, believes that Australia's quality is the best but that we don't advertise or market effectively compared to our European rivals. 'Australians will put a first-class product in cheap one-dollar packaging. This is a bad strategy as Russians are really big on presentation. Furthermore, once you get them, they'll stick with your product forever,' he says. Of course, Sergey Cherny's comments were reflective particularly of consumers in his hometown of St Petersburg. A short walk around the city certainly demonstrates the Russian emphasis on presentation. Peter the Great built St Petersburg 301 years ago to show Europe that Russia was its match in aesthetics. There are many wonderful buildings full of fine works of art, the highlight being the Hermitage.

Speaking of art and high culture, it was actually in Moscow and not St Petersburg that the airport economist witnessed a most unusual event when he was invited to an Australian Aboriginal art launch at one of the capital's trendiest cafes. On walking through the door and being confronted by a group of Russian models daubed only in Aboriginal-style body paint (they were demonstrating cosmetics), the airport economist thought he was at the wrong event. But low and behold, about half an hour later, the doors were opened and in came the 'A list' of the glitterati and literati of Moscow. It was a real case of Pushkin meets Pitjantjatjara. Whilst the new-rich oligarch men tried to negotiate buying the highly regarded indigenous art almost 'by the dot' (finally bringing wads of greenbacks out of their bulging pockets when told Aboriginal paintings had sold well at Sotheby's in London recently), their girlfriends went straight for the body-painted models to buy the Australian cosmetics. It was a great piece of product placement by the organisers of the event, who clearly knew the Moscow market well. Similarly, wine and food shows have been coupled with Aboriginal art exhibits as a way of building the Australian brand. And whilst changing tastes are attracting more Australian winemakers to Russia, the product is still the preserve of the newly wealthy—many of whom you will find at joint Aboriginal art/cosmetics launches.

The week I was there, St Petersburg was all abuzz as Paul McCartney was playing a major concert, but it wasn't Sir Paul's only visit to Russia in recent years. In 2003 he played to a sell-out concert in Red Square, in front of the Kremlin wall and St Basil's cathedral. And yes, he played *that song*—three times, in fact, to an excited Muscovite crowd, and accompanied by none other than President Vladimir Putin on the final encore. With the resurgence of the Russian economy and the opportunities in energy and consumer markets, it seems Australian exporters can safely get back to the (former) USSR.

13 A CHIP OFF THE OLD BLOC?

The expansion of the European Union has now brought in many of the old eastern bloc countries once hidden behind what Winston Churchill dubbed the 'Iron Curtain'. In the 'New Europe' the airport economist experiences the youthful energy of countries held back for decades by political oppression and some crazy examples of central planning.

ON MAY DAY in 2005, the European Union (EU) admitted ten new members to the club. With much fanfare, the EU leaders gathered in Dublin to celebrate EU 'enlargement', while more parties continued in the capital cities of the accession members. These really were amazing scenes given that most of the new accession countries were well and truly part of the Soviet sphere of influence only a decade and a half ago, with no institutions associated with liberal democracy or a market economy. Having come a long way in a short period of time, the new members are now part of the largest trading bloc in the global economy, and the EU's population has increased from around 378 million to more than 455 million. This has created a consumer market larger than Japan, Canada and the USA combined. Indeed, the enlargement of Europe is a pretty significant development for all Europeans, both old and new—and, for that matter, for the rest of the world.

But in the EU elections held a year after accession, voters in the 'New Europe' showed similar characteristics to those of 'Old Europe', with a low turnout and a large anti-incumbent swing. It seemed that whilst many people in the accession states were excited about the opportunities EU membership and a market economy offered, and about the entrepreneurial possibilities that were coming their way, they were still prepared to give the European politicians a kicking at the ballot box.

This was not what was 'supposed' to happen according to the Brussels officials who had sent me packing to the new accession states and the European mission to Australia and New Zealand, which was keen for me to witness the grand European project first hand in 'wannabe' member Romania (which did gain entry in 2007, along with Bulgaria). Scanning the emailed invitation to an 'Enlargement conference', I had to double-check before realising it was an official EU event—an occupational hazard in the 'spam age'.

The invitation came about because the trade press in Australia was dominated by the dispute over agricultural subsidies stemming from the EU's Common Agricultural Policy (CAP). This had been highlighted by a report in the *Business Review Weekly* stating that for the price of the EU farm subsidies, you could send all the cows in France around the world twice in business class. The picture that accompanied the article, with many cows surrounding the Eiffel Tour before boarding their plane (obviously not in cattle class), didn't go down well with the European mission or in Brussels. The mission clearly wanted some better news about Europe coming out of Australia. It was worried that Australian business had 'Europhobia' and wanted them to have 'Eurovision' instead, to take advantage of the opportunities offered by an enlarged EU. As a result, off went the airport economist to the former eastern bloc.

Revving up Romania

First stop was Bucharest. The airport economist had always wanted to go to Romania, mainly because of my 'blood' ties with the country. I used to think my father was joking about us being Transylvanian, maybe to get some interest going in the playground. But it's all true: my great-grandfather, Israel Harkowitz, came from Transylvania (now part of Romania, then part of the Austro-Hungarian empire) to Sydney in the 1880s. (As I've mentioned, his son, Kopel, changed the family name to Harcourt, which makes people think I'm French and works wonders in Paris—and, surprisingly, also did in Bucharest, which has a strong affinity with all things French.) Of course, the airport economist is also Polish, German, Lithuanian, English, Irish, Scottish and French (and has an American wife and a Chinese daughter), but it's the Romanian bit that gets the most interest.

For some reason, Romania has always had a bad reputation. Guide books talk about the stray dogs, roads full of potholes and some appalling architecture (former communist dictator of Romania Nicolae Ceausescu had a thing for massive Stalinist buildings). I remember being in the USA in late 1989, visiting relatives in Las Vegas, when Ceausescu was ousted in a bloody coup. My dad's cousins were in show business (spread all over Hollywood and Vegas) and one of them, Georgie Baker, was interested in the genealogy of our family. 'You know, you're Romanian, Tim,' he said. 'I think your great-grandfather—who was my grandfather—was a count or something. Maybe you could go back there and run the place.' But at the moment Georgie made this suggestion, I saw an image on CNN of Ceausescu and his politically powerful wife, Elena—they had been captured, tried and executed by the revolutionary regime in under forty-eight hours. Sure, it made riveting live TV—much better than *Big Brother*—but the bloody sight of the former dictator and his wife lying dead in the snow did not make me all that keen on a new political career in Romania.

Despite all these images, on finally reaching the land of his ancestors the airport economist found Romania to be a fascinating country, with a warm, open culture—more Latin than Slavic, keen to look to the west and with a population wanting to forget the excesses of the past.

And there were some good economic signs in Romania as it prepared to join the EU. The airport economist spoke with Deputy Governor of the National Bank of Romania (the central bank), Harvard-trained Cristian Popa, who is upbeat about the nation's macroeconomic prospects. 'We have just achieved 6.1 per cent GDP growth in the first quarter this year, up from 4.9 per cent last quarter (year on year), exports are up 17 per cent and, like all western central banks, we have a strong policy regime of inflation targeting,' he says. Popa's enthusiasm for inflation targeting, he explains, is a result of reading a study on the topic by the Reserve Bank of Australia's Guy Debelle and closely following the experience of Australia, the UK, the USA and other western economies.

But is this 'Romanian renaissance' providing new business opportunities for Australia? Surprisingly (to some at least), there is a vibrant expatriate community, enough to make up the numbers for the Transylvanian Cricket Club! One leading member of the Australian community in Bucharest, Andrew Begg, runs *Vivid*, a magazine for expatriates in Romania, which has really taken off. Begg says, 'With the increased numbers of westerners moving into town, I thought the time was right for a new type of magazine that talks about national and international politics, but also lifestyle issues plus the usual quota of local gossip. We've been overwhelmed at the response.' Begg expects to return to Australia 'eventually' but, at the moment, 'I'm having too much fun here with all the excitement. And I don't get too homesick,' he says. The Australian expatriate activities include some religious ceremonies, too. 'A group of us get together for the AFL grand final each year—no one's allowed to know the score, and we watch the taped game as

if it were live at 2.30pm Saturday afternoon in Bucharest!'
says Begg.

Another Australian expatriate works for an Italian
software company, which has its head office in Milan. He
finds it easier working in Bucharest than in the firm's other
offices in Western Europe. 'Romanians are keen, flexible and
always wanting to give it a go. They have none of this old-
world "been there, done that" weariness,' he explains.

Australians also do well in professional service firms in
Eastern Europe. Australian Garry Collins is a partner at Ernst
& Young's Southern and Eastern European office in
Bucharest. Collins came to Romania in 1995 after six years
in Budapest and three years in London. 'I found it more
challenging to be here than in the UK, which is so similar to
Australia. After years of communism, these countries are
learning about accounting standards and corporate governance in a market economy. It is very interesting and
stimulating work,' he says. Collins also finds the lifestyle
appealing. 'After the hassles of London, Bucharest is a really
easy place to live, and the countryside—particularly in Transylvania—is just breathtaking,' he explains.

So with Romania having finally joined the European club
in 2007, will things get even better in Bucharest? The World
Bank has been cautiously optimistic, and the National Bank of
Romania thinks the domestic economy is faring pretty well. The
development of infrastructure, skills and training is key, with
good opportunities for foreign consulting and engineering
companies (including Australians) who are willing to give it a
go. After all, Romania's human resources are there to be developed. Liviu Buzila, a local business consultant with strong ties
to Australia, agrees. 'Remember, we are a Latin not a Slavic
people; we grew up speaking English and French like the
Dutch. And we are well-educated—we have the second highest
number of IT specialists in Eastern Europe after Russia,' he says.

So there's some local optimism and, given the legacy of
Nicolau Ceausescu, you have to give the Romanian people

credit for bouncing back. But when it comes to political leadership, the airport economist, despite his bloodlines, will leave it to the new generation of Romanian democratic leaders to sort out.

Poles apart

Next stop on the eastern bloc express was Poland. Now, the Poles had given the EU a *real* kicking at the EU elections. But why? After all, Poland is a pretty big economy with a strong agricultural base and has everything to gain from EU membership.

Part of the reason is the overall distrust of the political process in Poland. The centre-left government was struggling when I visited, and the opposition wasn't faring much better. But the rightist anti-EU nationalist 'self-defence' party did exceptionally well—particularly in rural Poland.

However, the political scene seems not to have adversely affected the climate for investment in Poland, which remains attractive to overseas capital. GDP is growing at over 4 per cent, inflation is less than 1 per cent, fiscal policy is in good shape and the current account is around 2 per cent of GDP. Foreign direct investment flowed into Poland during the initial round of post-communist privatisations as Poland became the darling of free-market economics.

Some Australian names were included in that list of investors, including Amcor and Bovis Lend Lease. In fact, the Amcor cardboard manufacturing factory in Poland—which is the largest Australian investment in the country—has been so successful that its Managing Director, Jerzy Czubak, now runs all of Amcor Central Europe. Similarly, the property developer Bovis Lend Lease, the second-largest Australian investor in Poland, runs its Central European operations out of Warsaw and manages many state-of-the-art projects in the region. According to Jan Zyburski, the company's Central Europe Manager, 'We're very excited about Poland and about the whole Central Europe region. This area is really buzzing and is teeming with well-educated, talented people who could do the same job anywhere in the world.'

Indeed, foreign investors like Amcor and Bovis Lend Lease have remained in Poland on the strength of its initial privatisation programme and the overall strength of its economy. This has occurred even though other Central European economies are now attracting their share as well. But Polish unemployment is high—almost 20 per cent of the labour force. In fact, when some nice young Polish graduates kindly picked the airport economist up at Krakow Airport, their first question was not about kangaroos and Nicole Kidman but: 'What is the unemployment rate in Australia?' They were thinking of travelling to London (a real magnet for young Poles and Russians), and a couple had also started their own businesses. For instance, one young Polish entrepreneur, Slawomir Jackowski, has a travel and photography business in the wonderful medieval university town of Krakow. He regularly takes Polish tourist groups around outback Australia and his studio is covered with pictures of Coober Pedy and Andamooka. Imagine that, in the middle of Krakow!

The chronic state of the Polish labour market has actually provided opportunities for Australia. Whilst in Warsaw, the airport economist met with Lindsay Frost of NeoProducts, an Australian company that provides electronic employment kiosks for job seekers. NeoProducts achieved great success under the Blair government's employment programme in the UK and were venturing further into Europe for new contracts. 'We want to do our bit to find Polish workers a job,' says Frost. 'It'll be hard, but after our success in the UK—particularly in high unemployment areas in Scotland, Wales and the north of England—we feel that we have some runs on the board,' he explains. NeoProducts is also targeting the Czech Republic and other countries in Central Europe.

Czech mate!

The next stop was Prague in the Czech Republic, considered by many to be *the* centre of Europe now. With its magnificent castle and the Charles Bridge, many westerners flock to the Czech capital for business and pleasure. Prague was the stage of two famous anti-communist uprisings. The first was the ill-fated 'Prague Spring' in 1968, led by Alexander Dubcek and put down by Soviet tanks. The second was the successful 'Velvet Revolution' in 1989, led by famous Czech playwright Vaclav Havel. After the latter uprising and the division of Czechoslovakia into separate Czech and Slovak republics in 1993, the Czech Republic soon became the poster boy of the ex-communist states.

According to Petr Vodvarka, of the Australian Consul-General in Prague, 'We had the Velvet Revolution, but the Slovaks had the old guard still in charge. They opposed foreign investment and refused to open up Slovakia to trade and commerce. Of course, as a result, the Czech economy benefited immensely [from separation] in the early 1990s.' This enabled many western companies to set up in Prague, eschewing Bratislava (capital of the Slovak Republic). A notable early Australian success story was Cochlear, producer of hearing implants, which set up shop in the Czech Republic, as did Gosford-based Starena (manufacturer of stadium seating for Prague's Oparva stadium), and wine and sheepskin producers. According to Petr, 'Prague was one of the first cities to attract western-style hypermarkets, full of consumer products (many of which were Australian) that were new to communist countries. Also, the Czech Republic's manufacturing base and openness to foreign investment helped with auto components and advanced manufacturing goods.'

But now, after a change of regime and with it a brand new attitude to trade and foreign investment, the Slovak Republic has caught up and is often mentioned not just by the Czechs but also by the Poles as a major competitor for foreign direct investment. For example, Sebastian Mikosz, Executive Vice-President of the Polish Information and Foreign Investment Agency, was concerned about the loss of a factory by South Korean car giant Kia to the Slovak Republic.

Hungary for opportunity?

After Czeching out of Prague, the airport economist moved quickly to Budapest, capital of Hungary. Despite the Romanian connection, my father used to point out that Transylvania was really Hungarian when his grandfather left. He also used to say that the Hungarians are geniuses, so it might have been a matter of getting with the strength. Many Hungarians have done well in Australia—just think of business giants Frank Lowy and Peter Abeles and the legendary SBS football commentator Les Murray, to name a few. The old saying goes that if a Hungarian comes in behind you in a revolving door, they will end up in front of you by the time you come out. The Hungarians put great emphasis on education—particularly in maths and the sciences—and many Hungarian émigrés have won Nobel prizes. Hungarians make excellent economists, too. In the 1960s and 1970s, the British prime minister Harold Wilson employed two Hungarian economic advisers, Nicholas Kaldor and Thomas Balogh, who for reasons of respective physical size and temperament were known as 'Buddha' and 'Pest'.

But how does all this display of genius help Hungary now, a small country of 10 million people wedged between Austria and the east? According to economist Miklos Szanyi, of the Institute for World Economics at the Hungarian Academy of Sciences, Hungarians are 'great scientists and mathematicians, but still need other skills in terms of the management'. His colleague Kalman Dezseri agrees: 'We have many individual entrepreneurs but we need assistance and skills in managing our enterprises, which is one legacy of communism.'

Erika Palfi, of Austrade Budapest, points out that Australian companies are filling that gap, particularly in the services sector: 'Young Hungarians are very keen on Australia, and want to go there for work experience and study as well as a good time socially.' One of Erika's younger clients is Pap Istvan, the Hungarian-born manager of Sydney Apartment Hotel, a Budapest-based business owned by Australian hotel chain Medina Apartments. 'I love working for an Australian business,' says Istvan. 'In my industry of hospitality, Australians are very well-trained and have excellent management skills. They are good at service without being *servile*, which is well-respected by Hungarians, who are very independently minded people.' Istvan believes that there is a lack of mid-range tourist and business accommodation in the former eastern bloc, and Australian companies like Medina would be able to fill the market gap. 'Take Russia, for instance. It's either five-star hotels in Moscow or nothing. Australian hotels could do very well—particularly in the management and staff training aspect—just like Medina has in Hungary,' he says.

So after this jaunt, the airport economist did in fact discover that it is a new era for the economies of the former eastern bloc. It is an exciting time, but one not without risks. The major challenges seem to lie in institution-building and enacting cultural change. Whilst communist economies were good at producing many excellent mathematicians, scientists and engineers, management training and the skills required to thrive in a market economy are still lacking. There are also major infrastructure needs, particularly in countries like Romania.

But many Australian companies both large and small have dipped their toes into the new Europe, and their youthful energy and enthusiasm for entrepreneurship and education—along with a thirst for knowledge about seemingly exotic, faraway places like Australia—mean there were no chips in this bloc, but plenty of optimism despite the difficulties of the past. In addition, Eastern Europeans are incredibly friendly and affectionate. I noticed that female colleagues would often kiss you on the cheek as a greeting, and the number you got changed depending on the country. After realising this I asked Ana, a colleague in Warsaw, 'You know, the further I have moved east, the more kisses I am getting— is this custom?' She gave me a smile and a wink and replied, 'Just wait until you get to Vladivostok!'

14 THE ITALIAN JOB

What is the Italian obsession with Perth-born model Megan Gale? And how do Australian businesses take advantage of this? The airport economist travels to Italy to see the 'Gale force' sweeping Milan.

MOST OF THE time, we economists call interest rates for a living; others undertake cost-benefit analyses, seasonally adjust labour market statistics or calculate gross domestic product. However, occasionally even an economist gets a different type of task to perform. Whilst on my mission to the eastern bloc, the airport economist received an unusual call. I was asked to interrupt my programme in Bucharest to leg it—*pronto*—west to the Italian fashion capital of Milan, in order to interview Australian supermodel Megan Gale at the European launch of a new Australian skin care product. The launch was a key part of Australia's export effort into the notoriously difficult (and sometimes temperamental) Italian market.

How did this come about? Well, it all started in Megan Gale's hometown of Perth with Ganehill Pty Ltd, a new exporter of suncare products. As part of Austrade's new export-er development programme, Ganehill wanted to promote its

products in Europe and picked Italy as its key launching pad,
hoping to take advantage of Megan's high profile there.
Austrade Milan's Alessandra Orsini helped find Italian
distributors and importers and approached renowned
department store La Rinascente to stock the brand. 'La
Rinascente is a famous name in Milan,' says Orsini. 'The
store was established in Milan in 1865 by Ferdinando
Bocconi as Italy's first department store and has not looked
back since. Famous designers, photographers and literary
figures such as Marcello Dudovich, Fabrizio Ferri, Emanuelle
Pirella, Max Huber, Pier Paolo Pitacco and the (sometime
Australian) late Helmut Newton have all been associated
with the store.'

The idea to get Megan Gale was a masterstroke. According to Australia's Trade Commissioner to Italy, Amanda
Hodges: 'The Italians just love Megan here—they can't get
enough of her. Her down-to-earth Australianness goes down
well along with her beauty and great sense of style.'

After touching down in Milan and heading to my hotel
near the main square where La Rinascente is located, I'd
have to agree with her. Megan Gale seems to be everywhere I
go in Italy, on billboards for global mobile carrier Vodafone,
and the appointed Australia's 'tourism ambassador' for
Tourism Australia (I assume the campaign's creative direc-
tors thought Megan's image more enticing to Italians than
Paul Hogan's shrimps and barbies).

Making my way down to La Rinascente, there seemed to
be an incredible build-up to the big event—a bit like a major
match between AC Milan and its bitter rivals Inter Milan.
I guess Megan Gale coming to town from her European
home in the Italian-speaking part of Switzerland is a big deal
in Italy. The security would have given a G8 summit a run for
its money, and there were paparazzi everywhere.

But luckily the airport economist has an 'in' as Megan's
agent, Stefania Castaldi, has lined up an interview for me.
I also have a mission, as we say in Italy, 'for the family'. My

elder sister, Wendy, a development specialist, has lived in Rome for two decades and has an Italian husband, Claudio, and two little girls, Caterina and Emma-Claire. Kids being kids, the girls were getting teased at their Rome primary school for being half-Australian, so Wendy thought a photo of the immensely popular Megan Gale with Uncle Tim would do wonders for her daughters' playground popularity. I sent this request to Megan's people ahead of time, hoping to attract sufficient sympathy as well as a 'local connection'.

By launch time there were so many people crammed into the department store that the event kept being moved from floor to floor in an attempt to avoid a crush. I wasn't born when the Beatles came to Australia in 1964, but this is perhaps what it might have been like, except for the Italian accents and a 'fab one' being pursued instead of a 'fab four'. Excited schoolboys shoved their way to the front, teenage girls were dressed as mini-Megans, and old Italian men were declaring their love for Megan and kissing her hands, arms and anything else they could get hold of. In between all this pandemonium, Megan somehow managed to launch the Ganehill product, the crowd shrieking with delight when she occasionally mispronounced an Italian word or two (when you look as good as Megan Gale, you are clearly forgiven in Italy for the odd slip).

After the launch, I beat a retreat to the department store balcony for the press conference. Again thanks to Stefania, I manage to introduce myself to Megan in the midst of the mass of Italian fashionista photographers and writers. Taking in a rather dishevelled and un-Italian-looking economist sporting a blue suit and tape recorder amongst all the Italian glamourpusses and 'metrosexuals', Megan immediately says, 'Oh, you must be the Aussie guy whose sister has two little girls in Rome.' Silently thanking my nieces for getting me ahead of the hungry pack, I ask her what it is about Australia that Italians like, in her experience as the face of Australia in Italy.

Megan explained to me her role as Australia's Tourism Ambassador to Italy and how she was quite intimidated when she first arrived in the country. 'The first time I came here I was already famous. I remember coming into Rome airport and just having people following me and saying my name and I just came over here on a promo tour. The commercials that I did were such a success and it was a shock. I cried for a week because it was quite intimidating and quite scary as well, people jumping on you, grabbing you when you're not used to it,' she explained.

Fortunately, Megan has become used to her hordes of admirers in Italy and has used her profile to help benefit Australian exporters and to build the Australian 'brand' in Italy. 'I tell them about it all the time so I mean there's just so many positive points about Australia and I haven't met one Italian or one other person for that matter that's been to Australia and hasn't liked it or had a problem with it. But they say it's a bit like travelling to the moon. They think it's too far. Also, when trying to sell Australia to the Italians, as I do, I try to discourage a lot of myths there are about Australia. I mean, they all think that as soon as you go into the sea you're going to get eaten by sharks and that there's snakes everywhere. I mean, I've never seen a shark or a snake. I've never been bitten by a dangerous spider.'

'Not even in the modelling business?' I asked.

'I've been in very dangerous situations but luckily I've never sort of you know, suffered from anything like that.'

But with a few 'sharks' circling in the media crush behind, the airport economist decided to farewell Megan Gale before receiving a bite, safe in the knowledge that his nieces would be popular kids at their Rome primary school for some time as a result of this Milanese encounter with a Gale force.

There's no doubt that Megan's profile has helped Australian companies get a foothold into the Italian market. However, despite all this Megan Gale-generated excitement, Italy is a relatively small market for Australia. Australia exports wool, coal, zinc, wine, food and fast ferries to Italy. In return, Italy exports medicines, pharmaceuticals, machinery, household furniture and, of course, lots of fine clothes and fast cars back to Australia. Australia does have significant foreign investment in Italy, although Italy is a relatively small investor in Australia. Macquarie Bank owns 42 per cent of Rome Airport, Northsun has purchased gas licences in Northern Italy and Newscorp has interests in pay TV station Sky Italia. Larger Italian investors in Australia include Luxottica (which bought eyewear company OPSM), newspaper group Corriere della Sera, wine producers Antinori, Italian energy producer ENI, car giant Fiat (through its subsidiary Iveco) and Olivetti (banking and multimedia).

So will we get a Megan Gale-led export boom in Italy just like we got a Princess Mary-led boom on the back of her marriage to Crown Prince Frederik in Denmark? 'Given that Australia doesn't always register on the European radar screen, every little bit helps,' says Amanda Hodges. 'We're picking up a fair few small business clients in Italy, and the personal links certainly make a difference with over 800,000 Australians being of Italian descent and a further 30,000 Australians actually living in Italy.' This has helped in growing Australian businesses with an eye for the Italian market. According to Austrade research, there are almost 1300 Australian exporters to Italy, which is the fourth largest exporter destination in Europe after the UK, Germany and the Netherlands. Many are small businesses in manufacturing and services looking for 'niche' opportunities. Italy is also a happy hunting ground for many female-run small- and medium-sized enterprises.

In conclusion, the creative and innovative approaches taken by Australian companies like Ganehill show off Italy's potential as a significant market for niche rather than bulk exporters. But for the airport economist, the main lesson of the Italian job was that even if everything works well in theory, it's important to get out there in the real world of exporting and get some practical experience to really test your economic propositions. The Milan assignment showed that being the airport economist is a tough job, but someone has to do it.

15 BERETS, BAGUETTES AND BOARD SHORTS

French women don't get fat, so they can wear Aussie cossies. The airport economist discovers the lesser known surfing culture of France and an interest in Billabong, Seafolly and Rip Curl, miles away from Parisian couture.

BOARDIES IN BORDEAUX? *C'est impossible, n'est pas?* But it is *true.* Australian surf culture has a big following amongst young French people and brands like Billabong and Rip Curl are doing well all over Europe. Australia exports over $23 million worth of surfwear and surf-related products worldwide annually, and France is consistently the number one market in continental Europe. So it's no wonder that in the *Diplomat* magazine's Global 100 (a survey of Australia's top 100 global companies), Billabong earned more offshore revenue than Westpac. Australian surfwear exporters are doing a roaring trade amongst young French beachgoers (and even those who just *want* to be beachgoers).

Why the sudden interest in Australian surfwear in France? It's partially because of a strong surf culture in some of the beach regions of France that has also been replicated in Spain and even Cornwall in south-west England. A lot of it has to do with the rise in the Australian brand too, with

surveys from FutureBrand and GMI Anholt showing
Australia to be the number one 'country brand' in terms of
tourism, lifestyle and as a place to do business in. Simon
Anholt, the architect of the GMI Brand Index, believes that
there's never been a better time to capitalise on the world's
desire for all things Australian: 'Now is the time for Australia
to be producing great Australian-branded products, culture,
events, services, ideas and media as fast as it possibly can.
Anything that reflects, promotes and sustains those essential
and admired Australian values will sell.' A fair bit of this
'Brand Australia' is tied up in the major surf brands. Think
of Australia and for many consumers beaches and hence
brands such as Rip Curl and Billabong spring to mind in the
same way that Germany and BMW are linked, or Ikea and
Sweden, and Nokia and Finland. The French in particular
think of Australia as a young, laid-back country that empha-
sises lifestyle and an outdoor culture. That's one reason why
you see young kids wearing Billabong boardies in Bordeaux
and in the rest of France.

What other Australian products do well in France?
According to Kirsten Sayers, Australia's Senior Trade
Commissioner in Paris, 'It's a case of the three Fs—fish,
fashion and funk. Australian businesses are doing very well in
the seafood stakes, casual fashion and music and entertainment. We have clients ranging from rock lobster fishermen
to Mushroom Records.'

And despite France being well-known for its own cuisine,
many food products—including seafood, olive oil and
gourmet condiments—are actually imported from Australia,
and we have a good reputation amongst French consumers.
Perhaps the hit book by Mireille Guiliano *French Women Don't
Get Fat* should carry the subtitle 'Because they eat fresh
Australian produce and wear Aussie cossies'.

But are Australian exporters successful in France? For
many years, both Australian and French businesses have
complained about 'Channel fever': Australian companies will

jump on a Qantas jumbo at the drop of a hat and head to Heathrow, but it takes a lot of coaxing to get them across the English Channel to France and the rest of Europe. Some commentators even say Australian exporters have 'Europhobia'. After all, the expanded European Union (EU) has grown from a market of over 378 million people to more than 455 million. The new EU is an enormous consumer market that is larger than Japan, Canada and the US combined, yet Europe is hardly on the radar screen for Australian exporters. If you look at the top twenty destinations for exporters, only two European nations—the UK and Germany—feature, whilst large modern economies like France don't even get a guernsey. Although the DHL 'Export Barometer' did show signs of Australian exporters developing 'Eurovision' with some pick-up in export orders to Europe outside the UK.

But is there specifically a 'French problem'? When the airport economist spoke to pundits about the French election in 2007, many thought there was. France's brand new president, Nicolas Sarkozy, has vowed to shake up the French economy with some major economic and social reforms after a resounding election win. From the centre-right Union for a Popular Movement (UMP) party, Sarkozy has promised a mixture of free-market reforms in France's struggling economy, along with a major overhaul of the traditional French welfare state.

Sarkozy, who came to prominence as a tough-talking law and order politician, played a public and sometimes controversial role in the recent riots plaguing the outer suburban areas of major French cities, areas populated by disaffected and unemployed youth, many of whom were of African and Middle Eastern extraction. Sarkozy, himself the son of Jewish-Hungarian and Greek immigrants, became the focal point of a debate which began by looking at the economic problems of the deprived outer suburbs but evolved into one about French identity in a globalising, multicultural world.

To become president, Sarkozy had to defeat France's first female presidential candidate, Ségolène Royal, of the centre-left Socialist Party. The 'Sarko versus Ségo' match, as the presidential race become known, was like a regular Punch and Judy show, with some aggressive debating and tactics on both sides. Royal put up a strong showing, despite divisions within her own ranks on a whole range of levels. First, there was the philosophical divide between Royal's Tony Blair–like 'Third Way' modernisation policies and the more traditional European socialism of the rest of her party. Second, there was the complex personal partnership with Socialist Party chairman François Hollande (after being together for over two decades and rearing four children, their partnership was dissolved soon after the election). Finally, there were her *'bikini bleus'* as Royal, an attractive woman in her early fifties, was photographed in a swimsuit, which caused much controversy in a normally privacy-conscious France. Royal actually lost the women's vote to Sarkozy, 48:52 per cent, with some French commentators saying (perhaps tongue-in-cheek) that looking *too* good in a cossie may have cost her votes. Sarkozy is adding to his opponent's woes by picking the eyes out of the Socialist ranks in forming his cabinet. He is also backing Dominique Strauss-Kahn, a former Socialist finance minister, to be head of the International Monetary Fund.

So what is the new president's plan?

First, Sarkozy wants to improve France's macroeconomic position, especially given its stubbornly high unemployment rate of 8 per cent. On the fiscal policy front, he is trying to get some respite for France in the European Commission (which is perhaps an irony given that it was France and Germany who imposed the tight Maastricht Treaty fiscal restrictions in the first place, for fear of fiscal ill-discipline in the other EU nations). Sarkozy also has to counter the perception amongst French consumers that introducing the common currency, the euro, has been inflationary (a point disputed by European Central Bank economists).

Second, Sarkozy wants to overhaul the French education and healthcare systems to improve efficiency and accountability. Expenditure in these areas is contributing to the fiscal difficulties faced by France and there is concern that the education system is not creating what the French call the 'social ladder' in terms of equality of opportunity.

Third, Sarkozy has to tackle the French pension system, given the ageing of the population and the capacity of future generations of taxpayers to pay the social-welfare bill of the French state.

Fourth, there is the issue of the French labour market, which has undergone various changes in terms of working hours (including the 35-hour week and caps on overtime). Some economists, however, say that the French labour system may be more a symptom than the cause of the current malaise. For example, Nobel laureate Robert M. Solow has extensively researched European unemployment—particularly in France and Germany—and his empirical findings showed that the problem had more to do with the structure of capital markets and corporate governance in French and German business and banking circles than in their respective labour markets.

The labour market issue draws attention to widespread inequality in France, particularly between the prosperous, cultural inner city and the impoverished outer suburbs. The problems of the outer city connect closely with race and immigration as well, and in this vein Sarkozy has vowed a 'zero-tolerance on racism' policy after the Le Pen years (when xenophobic National Front candidate Jean-Marie Le Pen actually made the presidential run-off against former president Jacques Chirac in the 2000 election, pushing Socialist candidate Lionel Jospin into third place in the first round).

According to the French Trade Commissioner to Australia, Jean-Louis Latour, 'It is an exciting time in France, as the new president means business.' But in a joint French

Trade Commission–Austrade event in Sydney, he warned not to expect overnight success: 'There are great expectations on President Sarkozy—especially amongst the French people—to deliver on his reform package, but it is important to manage expectations as he has a mammoth task ahead of him.'

So what does the 'New France' mean for Australia? As well as the 'F words' mentioned by Kirsten Sayers, cultural exports are a growing market too. Australian indigenous art is doing well on the back of the new Musée du Quai Branley, with many French buyers also touring the Northern Territory. In addition, the hugely successful international music tradeshow based in Cannes, Midem, has provided an important international stage for up-and-coming Australian bands like Sneaky Sound System and The Audreys. Australian companies are also using France as an export hub for other French-speaking countries in Europe and North Africa (or at least where French is one of the main languages) such as Morocco. As Sayers explains, 'Morocco is rapidly opening up, as is much of francophone North Africa. Australian companies with expertise in infrastructure, tourism, agriculture, energy and services will find a booming market. Competitors from the EU and USA are already investing in these markets, but national governments and private companies are interested in looking at alternatives from "down under".'

Another opportunity for Australian exporters in France comes via sport. In the recent past there's been football, the Tour de France and the Paris Olympics bid, but hosting the 2007 Rugby World Cup brought many Australian businesses to France to leverage the opportunities available through some business-related networking. Austrade held Business Club Australia (BCA) networking functions in Paris, much as it did in the 2003 World Cup in Australia and at the Sydney Olympics. According to BCA's manager, Ashley White, the special event strategy for doing business has been developed over the last decade in both onshore and offshore forms.

'After the success of Sydney 2000 and the Rugby World Cup 2003, Austrade decided to expand its business networking programme at the Melbourne 2006 Commonwealth Games, Rugby World Cup 2007 in France, the FINA swimming championships and the Spring Racing Carnival in Melbourne before heading to Beijing in 2008,' he says. 'With few major international events in Australia on the horizon, it made sense to take the BCA model overseas.' Since its inception, BCA has held over 260 networking events in Australia and overseas. With around 8500 members (some 37 per cent located offshore), the BCA programme has facilitated over $1.7 billion in trade and investment deals since 2000. That certainly shows that the economics of networking—or 'the power of schmooze'—works in practice.

In rugby circles, the French are known to play with great style and flair but need a bit of structural adjustment in skill, game plan and tactics to actually win a World Cup. (They have been runners-up twice, whilst the French football team won the World Cup in 1998 and was an unlucky runner-up in Germany in 2006.) It's the same with the French economy: there's plenty of style and flair but a fair bit of structural adjustment needed for France to become truly internationally competitive again. There's clearly a lot of work for its new 'coach', President Sarkozy, to do.

So on your next trip to Paris, watch out for board shorts and Aussie cossies in France along with the great monuments and romantic bistros. And think about what could have happened if La Perouse had beaten Captain Cook to Botany Bay—we might all be spreading Vegemite on our croissants and tempting US audiences to 'throw another snail on the barbie'!

16 A TALE OF TWO WORLD CUPS

Friendly, humorous and laid-back—can this really be Germany?
That was the question asked by the airport economist on a visit to
Berlin. But when the united Germany hosted the FIFA World Cup in
2006, those sentiments about the hosts were shared by most tourist
football supporters (and, of course, the event was well-run too—but
we expected that!). After years of developing stereotypes from watching
Hogan's Heroes *on TV, the airport economist visited modern*
Germany to find a nation honestly confronting its past and looking
confidently towards its future.

ALL THE WORLD'S attention focused on Germany in 2006 as the
host of the football World Cup. It was Australia's first World
Cup appearance since 1974, also played in Germany but
during Cold War tensions and when our Aussie boys were
mainly part-timers. However, this time we had a well-oiled,
professional and star-studded team, led by master-coach Guus
Hiddink. And unlike 1974, this time Australia got to play in a
unified Germany, with no East versus West tension (both of
whom were in Australia's group in 1974), and with the now
united city of Berlin hosting an exciting final.

Many football fans commented on what wonderful hosts
Germans all over the country were in 2006—both friendly

and efficient—and on how enthusiastically the German people embraced their team, which played an exciting, fast-flowing game (thought to be very 'un-German' according to football stereotypes) under their California-based coach Jurgen Klinsman.

The confidence with which Germany hosted the final was also mirrored by the energy of the reunified country, in part through the restoration of much German architecture and civil pride in Berlin. Recently the airport economist had been mesmerised by film footage showing Berlin reduced to rubble at the time of Germany's surrender in 1945 on television programmes marking the sixtieth anniversary of the end of World War II. But on seeing the same buildings in newly restored, real life I could not help but think of how much destruction had been done—a lot of it self-inflicted—to an amazing city, capital of a remarkable civilisation.

Two world wars and the terrible, ideological struggle of the Cold War had certainly taken their toll on Berlin. The infamous Berlin Wall that divided communities and families in this city may have been torn down in triumph in 1989, but the airport economist found that there is still plenty of healing to do amid the fine efforts of architectural recon-struction and regeneration of the Berlin cityscape.

In fact, in architectural terms, in many ways it is the former communist East Berlin that has benefited most from rebuilding. There's the restored Potsdamer Platz and the new-look Reichstag (redesigned especially for the return of Berlin as the national capital after reunification). There's the Museumsinsel (Museum Island), where you can find an amazing collection of restored palaces, cathedrals and, of course, museums. The great German universities and other places of learning in both the humanities and the sciences are being restored as well. The architects of the new Berlin deserve credit for trying to introduce modern design blending the new with the old, whilst remembering

Germany's troubled past in an honourable way. It clearly has not been an easy task.

Berlin is also trying to rebuild its Jewish past with a new Holocaust Memorial, a new Jewish history museum and the Neue Synagogue. This was of particular interest to the airport economist, whose German-Jewish great-grandfather Daniel Gans (Gans translates as 'Goose' in German) fled to Australia to escape the storm clouds of anti-Semitism. Unfortunately, most of his relatives, based in the Frankfurt area, did not escape, and suffered the same plight as the six million.

But with all this architectural renewal, is Berlin's re-unification a reflection of the whole nation's? On closer examination, the airport economist found that Germany is still a tale of two economies or, at least, a tale of two labour markets. When the Berlin Wall came down, the reunified German administration didn't want to create two classes of workers, so the relatively high West German wages were applied across the board to the low cost–low productivity East while it made the transition to a market-based economy. Unfortunately, even a decade and a half after reunification, Germany is still experiencing labour pains with unemployment remaining the key economic issue. Manufacturing workers are increasingly worried about job security and employers are constantly calling for labour market reform. When the former German chancellor, social democrat Gerhard Schroeder, was about to hand over power to the conservative Angela Merkel, he agreed with some of her proposed reforms to work rules, although he did want to establish a minimum wage as had been done in the United Kingdom under Labour prime minister Tony Blair. (As Schroeder often pointed out, countries that make regular adjustment to the minimum wage and labour market protections—like Australia and Britain—have also experienced relatively low unemployment rates.)

But is there a 'German paradox' at play? Despite the calls for labour market reform, corporate profits in Germany are high and the profit share of national income has been growing. Why is this so? One explanation is that segments of German manufacturing production is either being relocated to the former East Germany, or 'outsourced' with EU enlargement to the Czech Republic, Slovakia, Hungary, Poland and other former communist nations. As a result, investment in Germany is low (as is local consumption) but German outward investment and German exports overall are high. In fact, the German predicament may well be one of capital flight rather than labour pains.

However, the consensus amongst EU economists in Brussels and at the European Central Bank in Frankfurt is that Germany is still playing the role of Europe's 'export engine room' and that its manufacturing exports, in particular, will continue to be an important driver in the European and world economies.

Is there a role for Australia to play in all this? To date, the Australian–German trade story has not been the most robust of all our trade relationships. In fact, Australian exports to Germany are at the same level they were at the time the Berlin Wall came tumbling down. On the other hand, the investment story is a good one, with historical links between Australia and Germany dating back to 1872, when the Siemens company supplied porcelain insulators used in the Overland Telegraph Line between Darwin and Adelaide. In fact, Germany is usually in the top five or six sources of Australian inward investment. Some big German names on the Australian corporate landscape (apart from Siemens) include Deutsche Bank in finance and Hochtief (owners of Thiess and Leighton Holdings) in the construction sector.

On the other side of the ledger, Australian investment in Germany is just over half the total of German investment in Australia. Many larger Australian corporates have established themselves in the German market: Amchor, Brambles, Cochlear, Qantas and Fosters are all there, and Macquarie Infrastructure is looking to expand its European presence in the German utilities sector. But there's plenty of room for more Australian companies to play a part.

According to Peter Rasmussen, Australia's Senior Trade Commissioner for Western Europe, based in Frankfurt, there are 2507 Australian companies exporting to Germany in total, which is the second most important European destination for Australian exporters after the UK (well ahead with 4808 exporters). Rasmussen believes that Australian exporters 'have made successful inroads into the larger consumer markets like food and beverage, but also in IT, advanced manufacturing and professional services'.

But there is more that can still be done. According to commentators in Germany, there is plenty of life left in the export engine room of Europe—and Australia has the potential to be a key provider of components in German manufacturing supply chains. For instance, Australian manufacturer Bishop Engineering produces high-quality, variable geometry steering components for Daimler-Chrysler from a factory in Saxony-Anhalt. According to Bruce Grey, Bishop's charismatic Chief Executive Officer, 'Australia has a good reputation in advanced manufacturing and German companies are keen to do more business with high-quality, competitive suppliers.' For the most part, however, Australian companies are focused on Asia and, with the rise of China and India, that could well continue. But there's no lack of demand from German industrialists for Australian products and know-how.

Let's hope that many more Australian businesses take up opportunities in German manufacturing and in the rest of the economy—just as the Socceroos took their opportunity at the 2006 World Cup. And as far as Berlin goes, may it continue to rebuild both its east and west sectors so it can start focusing on its future, as well as its past. Germany has certainly rediscovered itself and the time may be ripe for some Australian manufacturing exporters to do so as well.

17 THE KYLIE EFFECT

In the 1970s the United Kingdom was often described as 'the sick man of Europe', yet in more recent years it's 'cool Britannia' and the UK is one of the strongest economies in the world again. But no matter what the state of the UK economy, most Australian exporters make a beeline for London before venturing across the Channel or the Atlantic, just as pop sensation Kylie Minogue did (or the Easybeats, the Bee Gees and Rolf Harris did before her). The airport economist investigates the economic phenomenon which is known in exporting circles as 'the Kylie effect'.

REMEMBER WHEN ECONOMISTS used to describe the United Kingdom as 'the sick man of Europe'? This was usually coupled with the phrase 'the British disease' to refer to any sign of consistent economic underperformance and falling international competitiveness. How times have changed! In terms of economic performance, the UK is no longer the 'sick man' but the envy of the continent and one of the better performing economies in the OECD. 'The English patient', it seems, has made a full recovery, and is now sprinting to the head of the pack like one of those well-tuned middle-distance runners that Britain often seems to produce in the world of athletics (think Sebastian Coe, Steve Ovett, Harold Abrahams and the rest).

According to distinguished economics commentator Martin Wolf, the UK's resurgence is part of a growing trend of English-speaking economies outperforming the rest of the industrialised world. As Wolf has noted regularly in his *Financial Times* columns, the 'Anglo-sphere economies' have outperformed continental Europe and Japan regularly since the end of the 1980s. For example, in 2005 Wolf wrote: 'Between 1991 and 2004 (the trough of the US cyclical downturn before the slowdown in 2001), the gross domestic products of Australia, the US, Canada and the UK (in that order) rose considerably faster than those of France, Italy, Japan and Germany . . . GDP per head (at purchasing power parity) is similar. Between 1991 and 2004 it rose by 39 per cent in Australia, 32 per cent in the UK, 30 per cent in the US and 29 per cent in Canada. It rose by only 19 per cent in France, 17 per cent in Italy, 15 per cent in Germany and 14 per cent in Japan.'

In fact, Britain's economic performance has enabled London to consolidate its place as one of the major financial and political centres of the world economy. As Nick Cohen, a leading columnist for the *Guardian*, the *Observer* and the *New Statesman* has written: 'London is the only capital in Europe that is growing. At 7.3 million, its population is just short of the combined total of Rome, Paris, Vienna and Brussels. Another 810,000 are expected in the next decade as the rise of English as a world language and London's liberal reputation suck in more immigrants.'

In fact, London's ability to attract both capital and labour is one reason why the UK may not join its European counterparts in the common currency (the euro). The fact that the UK has outperformed the euro area to date may support the 'if it ain't broke, then don't fix it' sentiment of Britons who want to retain the pound and sovereignty over monetary policy. A large number of UK politicians also have similar views on the EU constitution.

Of course, this is not to say that the British are not 'good Europeans'. On the contrary, on the airport economist's first

visit to Brussels numerous officials and members of the
European Parliament commented on the excellent calibre of
UK representatives in the EU. For example, Michael Paulch,
a leading eurocrat in the EU's External Relations Direc-
torate, noted that: 'British officials are constructive,
professional and really help out committees in coming up
with practical solutions. They have a good reputation in
Brussels.'

So what does the UK resurgence mean for Australia?
According to Alison McGuigan-Lewis, Austrade's Senior
Trade Commissioner in London, the UK's image needs
some 'updating'. Just as the Blair government launched the
'Cool Britannia' campaign to promote Britain's cultural
renaissance, McGuigan-Lewis has worked hard to spread the
news about the thriving business environment that is providing opportunities for Australian businesses large and small.

'With Australia's recent love affair with Asia, contemplating business in the UK is perceived to be a bit
old-fashioned and "going back to Mummy",' she says. 'But
the fact of the matter is that the UK is still a great springboard
for Australian companies wanting to expand into Europe.'

And the economic evidence backs up her observations.
According to recent Austrade research based on Australian
Bureau of Statistics data, the UK is Europe's 'Top of the Pops'
as far as Australian exporters are concerned and that's where
'the Kylie effect' comes in. Just as Kylie Minogue and so many
others before and after her have done, London and the UK
still seem to be where you make your name and then build
on that into Europe, Asia and the Americas. When the airport economist was visiting London, the UK was attracting
4808 Australian exporters, light years ahead of second-placed
Germany on 2507. Then comes the Netherlands (1407),
France (1368), Italy (1215) and Belgium (753). Belgium and
the Netherlands score highly (relative to their size and
economic importance) because of the strategic positions of
the port cities of Antwerp and Rotterdam (playing similar

roles to Singapore and Hong Kong in Asia and Dubai in the Gulf region). For small- and medium-sized enterprises (SMEs) too, Britain performs strongly. According to Sensis, around 21 per cent of Australian SMEs export to the UK, which is second only to New Zealand on 44 per cent. As a result of this increasing interest in the UK from Australian exporters, Austrade is constantly expanding its networks in the UK and Ireland, with offices recently opening in Dublin, Edinburgh and Manchester.

So where are the gains being made into the UK market? Australia does pretty well in food and beverage, informational technology and professional services. The strong UK labour market has provided opportunities for Australian labour market services firms such as NeoProducts (which provides technology for employment kiosks and job-search firms) and gumtree.com (started by a group of young Australians and now one of the busiest employment and community websites in the greater London area).

Of course, Australian wines are the number-one import in the UK, having famously overtaken the French, but according to McGuigan-Lewis the average British household is seeing more than just our wines recently. 'In the British kitchen, you can find Australian cookbooks, kitchen utensils and high-quality foods; and in the nursery, Australian and Kiwi nannies are highly regarded,' she says. In fact, according to *The Good Nanny Guide*, a bestseller for UK publisher Random House, antipodean nannies are regarded as 'trouble-free, happy, sensible, reliable and fun to employ'. All this in the land of Mary Poppins!

In the living room, Australian entertainment does well. We know about the success of Kylie and actors like Cate Blanchett, but behind the scenes in the arts administrations of opera, ballet and galleries, for example, Australians also do well. In fact in response to a lack of local talent, the powers that be in the British arts scene are setting up an arts administration training college (in much the same way that the UK adopted the Australian cricket academy model). As McGuigan-Lewis says, 'The British often rate Australians more highly than Australians rate themselves.'

And don't forget the backyard! Despite the big difference between a traditional English garden and the Aussie back-yard, Australian company Jim's Mowing is one of the fastest growing franchise companies in the UK.

So the English patient is well and truly back on his feet thanks to economic reform and the Kylie effect. Let's hope that we see more Australian business action in the thriving British economy, both inside and outside London, so Australia brings back more than just the Ashes on a regular basis!

Postscript: Alison McGuigan-Lewis is now happily installed as Senior Trade Commissioner in Washington, DC and her successor in London is—wait for it—Kylie Har-greaves! No doubt we'll see a continuation of the Kylie effect for Australian exporters in the UK.

THE AMERICAS

18 ALL THE WAY WITH THE USA?

Australians seem to do well in Hollywood—look at 'our' Nicole, Geoffrey, Cate, Toni, and Russell (okay, so he's half a Kiwi)—but is that the case in the rest of the USA? The airport economist travels across the country to find Aussies thriving in all sorts of places, playing cricket in Chicago and schmoozing with stockbrokers in Manhattan and tech-heads in Silicon Valley along the way. He also investigates the 'battle for Seattle' and why the World Trade Organization talks broke down in the Pacific Northwest city.

DURING THE AIRPORT economist's first extended stay at graduate school in the USA in the late 1980s, George Bush was president, *Crocodile Dundee* was a hit (increasing the premium for Australian accents on college campuses) and Australians, although not well-known, were a curiosity to most Americans but generally well-regarded. On a trip to the US almost two decades later, I find George W. Bush is president; *The Crocodile Hunter* is a hit and Australians are immensely popular (mainly due to the late, great Steve Irwin and his wonderful love of Australian wildlife).

The first time around, US papers were talking about America's economic decline relative to Japan and Germany. This time, the economic focus is on the rise of the

English-speaking economies (the USA, the UK and Australia, in particular) compared to 'Euro-sclerosis' on the continent, and China has seemingly replaced Japan as the USA's main economic competitor. Of course, much has changed, notwithstanding the possible effects of the sub-prime mortgage issues in the United States which seems to be going from the sub-prime to the ridiculous in some circles. What lessons can I draw from these two trips about both the USA and Australia's business prospects there?

First, the USA is not a monolithic country, but diverse in terms of climate, community and business culture.

Second, Australians are making inroads in the US market at the big and small ends of the scale. This trend will continue thanks, in part, to better market access granted via the Australia–United States Free Trade Agreement (AUSFTA). This is because free trade agreements, in general, also help in terms of the *psychology* of exporting. Historically Australia has had a poor export culture, with low levels of export 'intention'. Free trade agreements therefore help raise awareness of trade opportunities in particular markets. For example, in August 2004 around 19 per cent of all exporting small- and medium-sized enterprises (SMEs) exported to the USA. By August 2006 (eighteen months after the free trade agreement came into force) it had risen to 27 per cent—just below the UK on 29 per cent and New Zealand on 40 per cent.

Third, Australians are well-liked and well-regarded in the USA (although these sentiments are not always recipro-cated). Australia's brand is always strong and we are regarded as a loyal friend (despite our accents rarely being understood or successfully imitated by the few brave Americans who try to do so).

The great diversity of the USA means that both large and small Australian exporters can play the game in the Ameri-can market. With an estimated 90 per cent of Australia's 44,000-strong exporter community overall coming from the

SME ranks, the airport economist found many Australian small businesses doing well in the US. Examples include a family-run business like Brookfarm in Byron Bay selling macadamia products to an increasingly health-conscious US market; John Kolm of Team Results providing motivational speaking services all over the USA (whilst authoring the kid's book *Crocodile Charlie and the Holy Grail*); and Lusty Threads, a three-woman business selling string bikinis in Florida.

From the big end of town, too, Australian companies are succeeding. Of course Westfield, News Corporation and Visy are well-known in the USA, but manufacturing companies such as Brisbane-based EGR are also doing well stateside. EGR supplies automotive parts and accessories to big names such as GM, Ford and Toyota in forty countries worldwide, with the US being a major export region.

So how to tackle such a large country? Given that the airport economist has lived in both Minneapolis and Boston (or technically Cambridge, where the Harvard University campus is) and is a regular visitor to San Francisco, this US trip took in three different cities—New York on the east coast, Chicago in the Midwest and Seattle on the west—with plenty of trips to the 'New South' as well in-between.

New York, New York

From a quick entree into the Manhattan cocktail scene by the airport economist it would seem that New York is the new capital of Australian expat life. Whilst London used to hold that crown—led by the likes of Dame Edna Everage, Germaine Greer, Clive James, Geoffrey Robertson and Kathy Lette—New York is now the place for ambitious Aussies to 'make it' (and if you make it there, you can make it anywhere). For instance, a dynamic Australian expat organisation called Advance enthusiastically provides personal services to Australian professionals in Manhattan and is expanding across the USA. According to Advance's Chief Executive Elena Douglas, 'Advance provides coaching, mentoring and matchmaking for Australian business professionals in the US across a range of sectors, from financial services to life sciences and the creative industries'. In short, Advance provides help with networking, job placement and education and training for Aussies moving to the States. 'We have strong links with important Australian business figures in the US like the Murdoch, Lowy and Pratt families, but also have US representation from big Wall Street firms like JP Morgan and Merrill Lynch.' Advance is joined in its work by the American Australian Association, which is also closely aligned with the elite of Manhattan business and political circles.

The influx of Australian expatriates to the Big Apple is partly a result of some clever negotiating during the time of the AUSFTA negotiations. In an unprecedented 'bonus', the USA created a separate visa category (the 'E–3' visa) specifically for 10,500 Australian businesspeople and professionals seeking to live and work temporarily in the USA. Australians with an E–3 can now work in the USA without needing employer sponsorship or having to enter the 'green card lottery'. In addition, their spouses can also work. Before this change the Australian quota was only 900, so Australians are now in a special position in the USA and many Aussies can follow Crocodile Dundee's example and take on Manhattan.

According to Andrew Stoler, Executive Director of the University of Adelaide's Institute for International Business, Economics and Law, 'This was a clever move by the Australian negotiators in Washington, a really classy performance. Australians are now getting very special access to the US market.' Stoler, a former deputy director of the World Trade Organization, also believes that this is just one example of how AUSFTA is a 'living agreement'. 'This is just the beginning—you can see how Australian professionals are increasingly going to get access to the lucrative US professional services market,' he says.

But there's always some who see a black cloud on every silver lining, and the great news about green cards is also being turned into a debate over whether we are suffering a 'brain drain' of expatriates. This 'expat problem' often seems to rage when one of our most famous examples, like Germaine Greer or Clive James, returns home and gives the rest of the citizenry a bit of free advice. And it's true, there are quite a few Aussie expats. According to Michael Fullilove (co-author of 'Diaspora: The World Wide Web of Australians', a new report on the expatriate community for the Lowy Institute), 'There are approximately one million Australians outside Australia on any given day. Perhaps three-quarters of these people—that is, as many people as there are in Tasmania and the ACT combined—are living on a permanent or long-term basis in a foreign country.'

But is there an expat 'problem'? Is it a 'brain drain' or 'brain gain'? Much of the talk about expats fails to see some of the positive aspects of having a strategic network of Aussies overseas, often in high and influential places or centres of knowledge and innovation. For instance, on the commercial side of things, having Aussies abroad can help our trade and business links. There are economic benefits to having around one million Aussies overseas when our total population is only around 20 million. Expats can help exports grow. According to Austrade research, 50 per cent of all new exporters enter international markets 'by accident', that is, through a chance meeting, networking event or over the Internet. Accordingly, 'clusters' of networks in major Australian export destinations are important sourcing events for new exporters.

The Lowy Institute's Michael Fullilove agrees. He says that the expatriates are 'a national asset that could be better utilised. Australia should take steps to engage the expatriate community more fully in our national life'. And in New York, that's just what Australians are doing.

Sweet home Chicago

The next stop for the airport economist was Chicago, unofficial capital of the great American Midwest. I had sporting business to attend to, but it was not the great American pastime of baseball—whether it be Wrigley Field for a Cubs game or southside Chicago where the White Sox reside—that interested me this time. Instead it was the seemingly un-American game of cricket. Whilst '20/20' cricket may be all the rage in the UK and subcontinent now, 30/30 cricket is well-established in Chicago. So how did we manage to get a sticky wicket in 'the Windy City'? It's all a matter of immigration. Out of a total population of over 8.5 million, the greater Chicago area is home to more than 200,000 Indians and Pakistanis, with a smattering of Bangladeshis, Sri Lankans, Caribbeans, Australians and New Zealanders. As a result, there's enough critical mass for a decent cricket match. According to New Zealand expatriate Richard Tattershaw, 'Every taxi driver here seems to be an ex-Test cricketer for Pakistan, or at least has swallowed a few Wisdens in their time with the amount of cricket trivia they can reel off.' To take advantage of this unlikely cricketing community, Tattershaw recruited a bunch of Aussies, Kiwis and even some curious Americans at an Anzac Day function last year. The team is known as the Fenders Cricket Club, named after P.G.H. Fender, reportedly the oldest international cricketer to attend (as a spectator!) the 1977 Centenary Test in Melbourne. Fenders play in a Chicago league against a number of strong teams from the Indian, Pakistani and West Indian communities.

But it should not come as a surprise that Chicago attracts so many diverse communities. After all, it has a hard fought reputation as a dynamic melting pot for immigrant communities from lands as far-flung as Poland, the Philippines and Puerto Rico. Chicago also has a reputation for being America's transport hub. According to Ian Smith, Australia's Trade Commissioner for Chicago and the Midwest, 'Whether you are talking planes, trains or automobiles, everyone comes through Chicago.' In fact, Chicago got its break one hundred years ago when the railways made the city their main cross-country terminus. The railroad companies didn't want to pay for bridges across the Mississippi (which harmed St Louis' chances, even though it was bigger than Chicago then) and Chicago's positioning was considered superior to Milwaukee's. And when air took over from rail, Chicago's pivotal role continued with O'Hare Airport. According to Mark Baillie, who heads Macquarie Bank's North America and Europe Real Estate Division in Chicago: 'You can get anywhere in America from O'Hare in a day's travel, and [its] global links are vital in my business, which stretches all over the continental United States, Canada and all of Europe as well.' Indeed, the official statistics support Baillie's observations: O'Hare Airport services forty-six international and an incredible 130 domestic cities with an average 3600 flights a day. And things are only going to get busier with a planned US$6.6 billion (A$8.8 billion) expansion, according to the *Economist* magazine's recent survey of Chicago.

Chicago's immigrant flavour and strategic position at the centre of everything has certainly affected its business culture. According to Richard Tattershaw, who runs graphic design company TimeZoneOne when not limbering up with the Fenders cricket team, Chicago is a relatively easy place for newcomers to do business in the USA. 'Chicago has a very open business culture which matches the Australian and New Zealand culture and temperament. My company, TimeZoneOne, makes 70 per cent of our design in Christchurch but makes all of our sales calls from Chicago. And they tend to like us. Basically, Aussies and Kiwis are regarded as having the sophistication of Europe but the hands-on practicality of American business, particularly here in the Midwest,' he says.

Australian Ian Greig agrees. Greig, who is also a Fenders cricketer, heads the Technical Division of Run Energy, a fully

Australian-owned company which provides operations, main-tenance and technical services to the energy sector. Run Energy started with three employees in 2003 and now has over forty servicing the USA, Europe and Australasia from its US base. According to Greig, 'Doing business in Chicago has been great for Run Energy. Chicago fits nicely into the different time zones of Europe and Australia, enabling an 'always online' approach. Run manages all its IT support and software services from Chicago. Being a web-centric company, Run is able to support its global team and customers with a click of a button,' he says.

Another Australian IT company, Systems Union, has had a similar experience. Director of sales Darren Goonawardana has recently moved to Chicago from Sydney and finds the local environment very conducive to running his business. 'The Australian brand is strong in Chicago,' he says. 'Australia is regarded as being good at high-quality inno-vation technology and has a supply of good-quality technical people. There's also a few "warm and fuzzy" things. They like the Australian manner at work and at play.'

But it's not all high-tech stuff. The Midwest is also a centre for more traditional industries like agribusiness as nearly all the Midwest's agricultural produce passes through Chicago on the way to world markets. For example, Nufarm (a major international agricultural chemicals company) runs its Americas division out of Chicago. According to Greg Crawford, Nufarm's General Manager for the Americas division, 'We are the only Australian multinational agricul-tural chemical company in the world and we're proud of it. Australia is well-regarded amongst the farming folks in the Midwest and we've developed some great relationships through our Chicago base.' Crawford also sees the free trade agreement adding to Australia's strong brand recognition in the US market. 'The trade agreement has helped our customers a great deal, which indirectly helps us. It has probably saved us a million bucks directly, too,' he says.

And Chicago is a major manufacturing centre as well. One Australian company, TZ Group, provides Australian-invented 'intelligent fastening' technology and has prospered since basing itself in Chicago. TZ's Chief Executive Officer, Chris Kelliher, says, 'In Chicago, we have great access to skilled and innovative engineers close to our partners and customers and, most importantly, to capital markets, an important factor for ongoing growth.' TZ is an excellent example of an Australian manufacturing company that has grown strongly in the ever-competitive US market. 'In 2003 we had thirteen people working for us, mainly mechanical engineers,' says Kelliher. 'Now we have over 160 people in eight international locations, with the majority being in Chicago. The company has grown faster than even our most upbeat expectations.'

Australia's influence also extends into Chicago's corporate sector. For example, Bovis Lend Lease is involved in building the Trump International Hotel and Tower (owned by world-famous property developer and reality TV star Donald Trump), which will soon be one of Chicago's tallest buildings, and Macquarie Bank has a quarter share of the Mercantile Exchange (which traded over one billion futures contracts in 2005 in everything from pork bellies to snowfall). According to Glenn Peters, Bovis Lend Lease's Australian-born Vice-president of Finance, Australian business culture suits the US construction industry: 'Australians are considered to be very practical and pragmatic. They are good at managing projects and finishing them ahead of time. While costs are controlled, there is no diminution of standards. In fact, at Bovis Lend Lease we have enhanced our occupational health and safety standards for our workers and have managed to lift our environmental standards too.' But it's not just projects like Trump Tower that brought Bovis Lend Lease to Chicago; the city is also important for overall positioning in the US market. As Bruce Watts, Bovis Lend Lease's Vice-president of Business Development, puts it, 'To be a national player, you have to have an office in Chicago.'

Mark Baillie says Australia is not only an important corporate player up and down the magnificent mile, but we are also increasing our influence nationally. 'Last year, Australia was the largest foreign investor in US corporate real estate. We are increasingly becoming a significant player. But unlike [in] a small market—like Australia and New Zealand—foreign investment can't distort the market [here]. It's also a very different scenario to Japan's experience of over-flooding in their market in the 1990s,' he explains. Of course, this can also have adverse effects given the impact of Centro on the Australian market.

Ian Smith believes that more Australian companies like Macquarie Bank, Bovis Lend Lease and Nufarm should consider Chicago as a base for their operations. 'There's no doubt that Chicago is an important national player,' he says. 'Chicago–Cook County [which encompasses the greater Chicago area] is an economic powerhouse in its own right with a population of 8.5 million people and a gross regional product of around US$370 billion. Whilst Australians gravitate to the coasts, they cannot afford to overlook the Midwest in terms of sheer market size and a business culture that's conducive to Australians, as evidenced by the success many companies have already had here.'

And, of course, expat staff for any Australian company basing itself in Chicago don't need to miss out with the presence of the Fenders Cricket Club. And this brings another advantage—a chance to look better than you do back home. According to Fenders' chief cricket enthusiast, Richard Tattershaw, playing away can inflate your performances and give you some good bragging ammunition. 'Someone who may be a scrubber in Sydney or Christchurch automatically becomes a champion in the Chicago league, so it's well worth it,' he explains. It reminds me of a conver-

sation I had with Professor Allan Fels when he was the head
of the Australian Competition and Consumer Commission.
After I complimented him on his cricket skills at a social
game, he told me not to be surprised as, after all, he 'topped
the state batting averages when he was a postgraduate at
university'. When I asked him in what state he was a postgraduate, he said: 'North Carolina.'

Sleepless in Seattle

Moving on to the west coast, the airport economist made his
first ever visit to Seattle in Washington state. There's something about this city that seems to attract big events in the
otherwise low-key world of international trade. In 1993, President Clinton hosted the Asia-Pacific Economic Cooperation
(APEC) Leaders Summit that really got the idea of an Asia-
Pacific community going. (Also memorable for former
prime minister Paul Keating having plenty to say about
another APEC leader, Malaysia's Dr Mahathir Mohamad.)
Then, in 1999, the World Trade Organization held its ill-
fated meeting, which ended with protestors and riot police
clashing on the city's streets.

So what is it about this rainy, medium-sized city in the
Pacific Northwest of the United States? What makes Seattle
so special?

First of all, this vibrant port city has always been an
international type of joint, a trading hub for the Pacific
Northwest. Seattle made its name as the last major port on
the shipping route to Alaska in the last century and as a port
for shipping lumber and manufactured goods across the
Pacific to Asia. Historically, prospectors had to prove they
had twelve months' worth of supplies before being allowed to
take on Alaska, so they stocked up at the Seattle markets first
(many also visited Seattle's red-light establishments near Pike
Place Market before undertaking the cold and lonely journey
north to the Arctic circle).

Second, Seattle has had its fair share of local companies which have gone on to bigger and better things on the international stage. There's the Boeing Company, the inventor of the jumbo jet, and, in more recent times, Internet giant Microsoft and global consumer brands like Amazon and Starbucks.

Third, known as a centre of innovation and creativity, Seattle is big in 'tunes, toons and TV'. Musically, Seattle has been home to many great blues and rock legends such as Jimi Hendrix, Ray Charles and Robert Cray, and the more recent emergence of Pearl Jam and Nirvana established Seattle's proud bragging rights as the birthplace of grunge. In cartooning, *The Simpsons*' Matt Groening and *The Far Side*'s Gary Larson first drew their quirky illustrations in the Emerald City. In television, hit shows such as *Frasier* and *Twin Peaks* were based in the city and its surrounds and, on the big screen, Seattle's fabulously scenic backdrop was on display in *Disclosure* and, of course, *Sleepless in Seattle*. In many ways, just like the 'it' girl, in the 1990s Seattle was the 'it' city.

So did the 1999 riots end Seattle's taste for globalisation? It seems not. Prominent Washingtonians and community leaders are still proud of the 'global' nature of the city, and it comes from both sides of politics. Washington State Governor Gary Locke, a Democrat, was America's first governor of Asian descent and is a vocal advocate for Seattle's place in the Pacific Community. On the Republican side, Jennifer Dunn, who until the election of Nancy Pelosi as Speaker in 2007 was the highest-ranking woman in Congress, is a known proponent of international trade and is co-convenor of the American–Australian Free Trade Agreement Coalition in Washington, DC. Congresswoman Dunn strongly supports the stake that Washingtonians have in international trade: 'From the major manufacturing and services companies in the Seattle-Tacoma area to our farmers in the east of the state, we all depend on trade for our livelihood,' she says.

So how does Australia fit into this picture? According to Congresswoman Dunn, there's a lot of interest in Australia in the Pacific Northwest. 'Washington State itself is a major trading partner with Australia in its own right. By volume, Washington is the nation's largest exporting state to Australia at US$2.6 billion—well ahead of California, Illinois and Texas. Australia is the fourth largest destination for goods produced in Washington, accounting for 7.6 per cent of the state's exports to the world,' she explains.

And this is important for employment in the area—especially high-paying jobs. According to Congresswoman Dunn, 'Around 12,520 Washington State jobs depend on exports to Australia, and jobs produced by exporters pay 13 to 18 per cent above the national average.'

Local union leader Charlie Bofferding agrees. Bofferding, Executive Director of the Society of Professional Engineering Employees in Aerospace (which covers engineers and technical staff at the Boeing Company), makes the connection that 'if the US doesn't buy Australian beef, lamb or dairy products, they won't have any money to buy Boeing planes . . . and that means less work for my members'.

And the Boeing Company itself sees Australia as a crucial market. According to Douglas Groseclose, Vice-president of International Sales at the Boeing Company: 'Australia is not only a great friend but a great customer. Australia is really doing something right in terms of its economy . . . it's a great market for us. Of the last eight Boeing planes we've sold, seven went to Australia.' And Groseclose is bullish about future prospects. 'Australia and New Zealand are just booming,' he says. 'We see great growth potential in that market, especially given their proximity to Asia.'

Of course, the FTA may also help Australian companies in Seattle. Recent Austrade research shows that there are almost 8000 Australian companies exporting to the USA and plenty of growth in areas open to trade like the Pacific Northwest. According to Len Reid, Australia's Honorary Consul in

Seattle: 'The FTA is going to give this healthy number of Australian exporters an even bigger boost locally. Australians have a significant—though low-key—presence in Seattle and do well in all the key areas, from aviation engineering to software programming and education.' Reid, a leading aeronautical engineer with Fatigue Technology Inc., has lived in the area for seventeen years. 'We have a lot of Australians coming through here in a range of businesses, but many get the "Seattle bug" and stay on. I still call Australia home but must admit that Seattle's attractions—from scenery to sports to culture activities—can be really addictive,' he says.

So it seems Seattle is a thriving, global city with plenty to offer Australia and other Asian-Pacific trading partners of the United States. With the expansion of Australian-US trade with the FTA, we may see a lot more action across the Pacific, particularly in the north-west. And with so much opportunity, Australian exporters just might find themselves to be 'sleepless in Seattle' for many years to come.

But are there any problems in going stateside? Sure, it's a tough and competitive place, although many Australians assume that because English is spoken it will be a doddle. As they say, an Australian exporter who avoids Asia for fear of losing his shirt may end up losing his pants in America (and that's not just confined to Memphis). Common problems include assuming the US is one big homogenous market when it is in fact incredibly diverse, as the airport economist's travels show. Another issue is intellectual property. For example, BlackJack Wines from Harcourt (no relation) in Victoria came up against Jack Daniels in Tennessee over naming rights (although the mediating efforts of Brett Henderson from Tradestart, Austrade's regional office in Bendigo, resulted in both companies sharing the rights). But who can forget Ugg Boot and the problems the Australian company had in the USA with its brand name? (A compromise was finally reached after a messy legal battle over competing trademarks.) In short, you have to do your homework when exporting to the USA despite language similarities, FTAs and their tendency to like Aussies.

The airport economist's whistlestop tour of the USA ended in Seattle, but I expect there will be many more. So from the perspective of my first US encounter in the late 1980s up to now, what can I expect to see in, say, 2020? By then, George P. Bush (son of former Florida governor Jeb Bush) may be president; Crocodile Bindi (Steve's charismatic daughter) might be hitting US digital screens, and Australians will no doubt still be popular in the US. But I expect that Americans, bless them, still won't be able to understand Australian accents.

19 BLAME IT ON RIO

Why is Brasilia the capital of Brazil when the business is done in Sao Paulo and the pleasure in Rio de Janeiro? The airport economist investigates this and other paradoxes in the amazing nation of Brazil. He is also an unwilling participant in a confrontation on Copacabana Beach with some surprising results.

THE AIRPORT ECONOMIST'S first visit to Brazil was to attend the World Social Forum, a sort of left-wing 'think tank'. It basically came about after global political and business leaders started meeting at World Economic Forum retreats in the Swiss resort town of Davos each year. In response, many development NGOs, environmental groups, trade unions and the like decided to organise a progressive forum to discuss issues of globalisation and take into account different perspectives. But instead of holding the forum at an expensive ski-resort town like Davos in a rich country like Switzerland, the organisers of the World Social Forum chose to meet in the developing world, with the first event held in the Brazilian port city of Porto Alegre, in the southern state of Rio Grande do Sul.

Whilst Davos attracts big-name movie stars and celebrities like Angelina Jolie and Sharon Stone amidst world leaders and financiers, Porto Alegre has its own sort of 'intellectual rock stars'. For instance, the famous American left-wing intellectual Noam Chomsky's appearances were standing room only and he was feted as a modern messiah of the left. This came as a surprise to the airport economist, who had been taught by Noam Chomsky in the USA. Chomsky was lecturing the 1999 class of the Harvard Trade Union Program and was regularly heckled as a 'commie' by some members of a relatively small but very vocal group of students. I was amazed when thousands turned out to hear Chomsky at the forum in Brazil, and thought it rather ironic that only a few years before we had had him all to ourselves but treated him rather disrespectfully. One thing I did know, though, was that he did go on a bit. If you asked him a question, he would give a book-length answer without interruption for about forty-five minutes. And he did so whether there were thirty trade-union students sitting in with him in Cambridge, Massachusetts, or 3000-plus social activists in Porto Alegre.

Apart from Noam Chomsky, another speaker I met at the forum was a metal worker union leader from the *favelas* (the shanty towns of Brazilian cities). He was a big fellow with a bigger beard, full of life and energy and with quite a large entourage. As I was at the World Social Forum as a guest of the International Labour Organization and had once worked for the Australian Council of Trade Unions (ACTU), I was introduced to him at a session we both presented on globalisation and the labour market. He said his name was Lula and I thought nothing of it, except that he seemed to be a character with a bit of 'go' in him, like most metal worker officials in Australia. It was only later that day, on noticing that my co-speaker knew a lot of people at the forum, that I realised that 'Lula' was in fact Luiz Inacio Lula da Silva, the Workers' Party (PT) candidate for the presidency of Brazil. That year, Lula indeed went on to become Brazil's president, leading the PT to victory and taking over from the two-term Social Democrat president Fernando Cardoso.

The forum had come to Porto Alegre after the state PT
government offered to host it there. I met the PT state
governor, who said: 'I would like to speak to you, but I know
no English. English is a language I will learn in my next life!'
I then confused the seminar's translation services by telling
the delegates to turn their simultaneous translation headsets
to 'number 5' (1 was for Portuguese, 2 was for Spanish, 3 for
French and 4 for English). I told them number 5 would
translate my talk from Australian into English and this
created chaos (even by Brazilian standards) as people leapt
to their feet demanding new headsets from the organisers.

I later retold the story about the translation mix up at my
hotel, which was full of officials from places like the World
Bank and the IMF, who had been banned by the organisers
from attending the forum. It must have been hard for some
officials whose whole job was to liaise with NGOs on behalf of
their institution only to find that they were locked out after
flying all the way from Washington DC to Porto Alegre. They
later asked me how come someone like me got in *and* was
able to give a speech as well. 'Who do you work for?' one
World Bank official asked. 'The Australian Trade Commission,' I replied, to add to the confusion of the day.

The forum lasted a week and, despite the diversity of
opinion present (though naturally with some overlapping
agendas), the energy was refreshing—the delegates had
their hearts in the right place and wanted to make a better
world. There were many cultural events, too, which added
plenty of festivity and colour and made the event unique (it
was no boring economists' conference, that was for sure). In
addition, many of the South American social activists dressed
quite unlike their counterparts in Australia, New Zealand,
Canada or the UK. A lot of the guys were in suits and ties
and many of the women in smart skirts, pant suits and high
heels, bringing together both 'fashionista' and 'feminista'
elements to one great cause. In fact the airport economist's
older sister, a leading feminist in Rome, always comments on

how members of the feminist movement in Latin countries always dress more elegantly than their counterparts in 'Anglo' countries. The airport economist asked one of the Brazilian delegates about this and she said: 'Of course, I dress well. They regularly televise these demonstrations and I want to look my best. Who wouldn't!'

After the forum the airport economist headed to Sao Paulo, the financial capital of Brazil and a massive industrial city of 20 million people. I find Sao Paulo intimidating and overwhelming, with no obvious physical attractions to speak of, but the locals—the Paulistas—swear by the place. It's where everything in Brazil gets done, they say, and as such most Australian business activity is centred on Sao Paulo. According to Gerard Seeber, Australia's Consul-General in Sao Paulo, Australia is increasing its involvement with the Latin American giant: 'Brazil has an explosive energy, and with its sheer size, in terms of geography and industrial capacity, there's plenty of scope for Australian businesses to get a slice of the action. Agribusiness, mining, food and beverage, infrastructure, environmental management and education are key areas for Australian exporters in Brazil in particular, and Latin America as a whole,' he explains.

Most Paulista businesspeople I met with were sceptical about Lula when I told them about our meeting back in 2002, but there has been more acceptance over time. Despite some initial market jitters, Lula has basically continued the fiscal responsibility shown by his predecessor as well as combining market-based reform with progressive social policies. As a result, Brazil has experienced falling unemployment and a steady growth rate of between 3 and 4 per cent per annum, which is about average for the Latin American region. Lula has also pressed for more trade negotiations—particularly within the Americas—and provided economic leadership within the region and at the World Trade Organization.

In the film *Blame it on Rio*, British actor Michael Caine plays an expatriate businessman who works and lives in Sao

Paulo but takes a holiday in Rio with disastrous consequences. His character comments at the beginning of the
film that Sao Paulo is where the work gets done, but Rio de
Janeiro is the place to play. Is this true? On arrival in Rio
de Janeiro, the airport economist saw plenty of action. There
were always masses of people at Copacabana Beach—day or
night, any day of the week—playing football or beach volley-
ball, and there were also street dancers practising for
Carnivale later that month. But the Cariocas (the locals of
Rio) also take pride in their city's commercial culture. After
all, Rio de Janeiro was the capital of Brazil before the in-
vention of Brasilia (located in the middle of the country so
as to open up the interior of Brazil in the 1960s) and, as a
result, it still packs some punch as a major international
commercial centre. Australian exporters to Rio have found
some success in light industry, education, tourism and
research and development in areas like biotechnology
and sports medicine.

But whilst Rio de Janeiro may be known for its sun, sand
and string bikinis, it also has a less happy reputation. Poverty
and gang-related violence in Rio's *favelas* have been well-
documented in many feature films, and the average traveller
to Rio usually feels a bit nervous on their first visit. Oddly
enough, the airport economist was himself a *cause* rather than
a victim of violence in Rio de Janeiro whilst, of all things,
jogging along a track around the Copacabana. At one point I
realised I was actually on a bicycle track (about the same time
I noticed a large Brazilian on a bike suddenly right behind
me). With the agility of an amateur league back-pocket player,
I tried to swerve out the way but collided with the hapless
cyclist, who somersaulted and landed on his knee, badly
cutting his leg and who knows what else, and snapping his
brand new bike in two. I don't know how it happened but
suddenly I could understand Portuguese perfectly: 'F*** you,
you silly f***ing gringo,' he said. 'Don't you know this is a
bike track?' And added (my translation skills still remarkably

accurate, I believe): 'I am going to f***ing kill you!' I
prepared myself for the worst as a crowd gathered, but the
local Cariocas must have sensed my hopelessness and turned
on my attacker—how would a simple gringo, a mere visitor to
Brazil, know about the track? After some pushing and
shoving, and even a bit of biff, the Rio tourist police arrived
to sort things out—and issued *me* with an apology! 'Please
come back to Rio, we like visitors—especially from Australia,'
they said. I took that to mean, including any stupid ones
who jog on the bike track and who can't speak a word of
Portuguese.

So that was Brazil, or at least Porto Alegre, Sao Paulo and
Rio de Janeiro, which is just scratching the surface of this
massive country. And how did Lula end up? In 2006, four
years after the World Economic Forum in Porto Alegre and
his initial victory, Brazil's first working-class president won re-
election. And this time, unlike in 2002, Brazil did *not* win the
World Cup, so there was no football fever to take political
advantage of (which is a *big* deal in such a football-mad
country). In 2006, Lula had to rely on Brazil's credentials
in economic performance, not football wizardry. Let's hope
Brazil's economic resurgence continues so that more Australian exporters 'go to Rio' in the future.

20 DON'T BUY FROM ME, ARGENTINA

One hundred years ago Argentina was richer than Australia, but now it's a different story. The airport economist investigates Argentina during its latest economic crisis to solve the mysteries of money, Madonna (playing the country's beloved Eva Perón) and, of course, football icon Maradona.

IN JANUARY 2002, the airport economist visited Argentina in the midst of a financial crisis. It was a fascinating opportunity for an economist to see how economic events interact with political events in times of crisis. In Buenos Aires there were endless demonstrations outside the famous Casa Rosada, where in the 1940s Eva Perón (once the beloved first lady of Argentina, often known by her nickname, 'Evita') addressed the massive working-class crowds ('the shirtless ones'). In fact, Eva Perón is still so revered in Argentina that there was a national outcry when Andrew Lloyd Webber's musical *Evita* was made into a film and Madonna was chosen to play the leading lady. Given Madonna's past controversies with sex, Catholicism, politics and every explosive issue in-between, the makers of *Evita* were not permitted to film in Buenos Aires and had to shoot the main scenes—particularly of Madonna playing Evita on the balcony of Casa Rosada—in Budapest. Any film export revenue that could have been deposited into the Argentine government's much depleted coffers therefore ended up in Hungary, but most Argentines said it was a matter of national pride not to denigrate the memory of Eva Perón.

However, in 2002, the masses were not showing the same adulation of their current political leaders as that shown in times past. In fact, the feeling was one of widespread hostility towards the political elites and a severe lack of trust and confidence in the country's economic and political institutions as a result of the financial crisis and the constitutional fallout from it. The massive demonstrations brought together gauchos from the country, workers and urban middle-class Porteños (residents of Buenos Aires) who had lost their savings and jobs and seen their businesses go broke. I was warned by locals not to walk around at night which surprised me, as until the crisis Buenos Aires had always been considered one of the safest South American cities.

So how did a once prosperous country end up in such a state? Current events do not reflect Argentina's past economic history. In fact one hundred years ago, Argentina was one of the richest countries in the world. In an interesting comparison, Buenos Aires and Melbourne both had some of the highest per capita incomes in the world and, like Australia, Argentina was rich in exportable commodities, had vast land to explore and settle, and became a wealth magnet for immigrants from the Old World. The phrase 'as rich as an Argentine' came into common usage. But today, the contrast between the fortunes of Argentina and Australia could not be greater. Australia is one of the most successful economies in the world; Argentina is plagued by a crisis of confidence with an economy in prolonged recession and marked instability in political governance. This has occurred despite Argentina's still considerable resource base and highly skilled workforce.

So what went wrong in modern times? Whilst Argentina does have a history of boom and bust, the most recent crisis concerned 'the three d's': dollarisation, devaluation and default.

First, let's look at dollarisation. To combat hyperinflation in the early 1990s the then president, Peronist Carlos Menem, pegged the Argentine peso to the US dollar. Unfortunately for Argentina, the strength of the US currency over the course of the decade left Argentina with an uncompetitive economy (contrast this to Australia which had 'floated' its currency, enabling the exchange rate to take the burden of adjustment instead of the whole economy).

Second, there's devaluation. The dollarisation policy eventually had to come to an end, but the subsequent devaluation of the currency became very unpopular as many Argentines (both businesses and households) held their debts and mortgages in *US dollars* whilst earning their incomes in Argentine currency. Argentines have had to face political and economic instability with bank restrictions, austerity measures and, eventually, the third 'd': default. The economic crisis has been accompanied by political instability with a series of presidents coming and going in quick succession. The Argentine people have had to endure half a decade of deepening recession with worsening unemployment.

How is this affecting trade? Despite the devaluation, there have been few benefits coming through for Argentine exporters, many of whom are still waiting for their export value added tax benefits. In addition, many Argentine exporters have to pay mortgages in US dollars. There are domestic considerations, too. According to Argentine economist Marianna Iribarne, 'Dairy and beef producers receive four-fifths of their sales from domestic markets and have been badly affected by floods as well as the unstable financial situation.'

The environment has also affected some Australian exporters (movie theatre companies Village and Hoyts, for example, have a strong presence in Argentina). Many foreign companies, including Australian ones, have been affected by having income streams in pesos but liabilities in US dollars.

So that's the bad news. Is there any good news?

Well, yes. First, despite the uncertainty and instability, the reforms introduced may improve Argentina's medium-term viability. This will, of course, depend on the institutional response of Argentina at economic policy and political levels.

Second, the devaluation has had two major effects. It's made Argentine exports competitive for the first time after many years of dollarisation, and it has also prompted a mini tourism boom in Argentina as Chileans, Brazilians, Uruguayans and Mexicans take advantage of cheap holiday deals.

Third, there may be benefits for some Australian companies who stick it out through the crisis. For instance, during the Asian financial crisis, the Australian companies that maintained their presence 'through thick and thin' benefited in the recovery phase. This could also occur if Argentina's situation improves.

One Australian case study is CHEP, part of the Brambles Group. The company is involved in the management and rental of industrial pallets and services clients such as Procter & Gamble, Colgate-Palmolive, Bayer, Nestlé, McCain Foods and a number of Argentina's largest retail and wholesale outlets.

Daniel Guerra, General Manger of CHEP for Argentina and Uruguay, believes that Australian companies, if patient, can come out of the crisis intact. Guerra regards Argentina's as a 'slow crisis' and draws upon the experience of colleagues working with other economic crises in Brazil and Mexico. He says success will depend on the skills of CHEP staff: 'The skills that are necessary to do business in normal times are not enough in times of crisis, such as we currently have. The first [extra] skill is to have the capacity to accept the reality of the situation—to look at it objectively and accept it, whether you like it or not. The second is teamwork—creating groups to analyse each subject. For example, having one group to look at the legal consequences, another group to focus on operations, etc. The third and most valuable skill is visionary leadership—if accepting reality is necessary, the vision is the lamp that will keep the team motivated and the company on the right track to reach its goal.' Guerra believes it is an opportune time to invest in Argentina and says 'enterprising companies with a business vision and developing the right segment will find that Argentina offers a strong growth potential which more developed markets don't have'.

On hearing Guerra's analysis, it struck me how important *trust* is in building relationships and therefore institutions in an economy. When Argentina's greatest football icon, Diego Maradona, was interviewed on television during my visit, he was asked which goal of his career was the greatest. His surprising answer was the infamous 'hand of God' goal in 1986 in Mexico, when he illegally punched the ball over England goalkeeper Peter Shilton into the net but made it look like an amazing (and, of course, legal) header. Yet, in that same game alone, which was a World Cup quarter final, he scored a brilliant goal when he dribbled the ball from the Argentine defensive half past nearly the whole England team in an amazing solo effort. But somehow, in a game that took his country into the semi finals of the 1986 World Cup, which Argentina later won, the 'cheat' goal was a prouder moment for Maradona than a goal showing his great class, skill and overall individual brilliance.

In a way this strange sense of priorities seemed to seep into Argentine economic and political life during the crisis, where there was more incentive to win by cheating than by business excellence and ordinary Argentines lost all faith in their institutions, whether it be the banks, the courts or the politicians. Fortunately, many Australian businesses had forged strong relationships of trust with Argentine businesses and customers, and made sure their partners knew they would stick with them through the worst of the crisis (just as many Australian exporters had done in Asia during the financial crisis of 1997–99).

So the bottom line for Australian business when it comes to Argentina? During a crisis, it's the quality of your business *relationship* that really matters. Relationships that succeed do so when trust is built up over time between the two parties. After all, as the airport economist learnt in Buenos Aires, in business as in life it takes two to tango.

21 RED HOT CHILE

After years of military dictatorship, Chile now has a democratically elected president who spent some years of her exile in Australia. The airport economist investigates the economic jewel in Latin America's crown that is Chile and finds some surprising developments that are benefiting both our countries.

CHILE IS CHANGING, and the fact that Chile now has a woman president is just the start. From the centre-left, Michelle Bachelet is a medical practitioner and has served as both defence and health minister in the cabinet of her predecessor, Ricardo Lagos. She is also a divorcee, which is very unusual in Catholic Chile where divorce has only recently become legal. Dr Bachelet also spent time in exile in Australia during the Pinochet years and has family links here with a brother in Sydney.

In fact, not only is participation in politics a new phenomenon for women in Chile but participation in the labour force, full stop. That was a key message of the Chileans the airport economist spoke to when visiting Santiago. According to Karen Poniachik of Chile's Foreign Investment Commission: 'Chile has traditionally had a low female labour force participation rate, but now with falling unemployment, we need to attract more women into the labour market.'

An improving labour market is but one of many impressive economic statistics notched up by the Chileans. According to Dr Sandra Manuelito, of the United Nations's Economic Commission for Latin America, Chile is the standout of the economies covered by the commission. 'Chile is undoubtedly the first world economy of the region. Of course, it has benefited from high commodity prices and therefore very favourable terms of trade, but its long record of economic reform and openness has helped as well. Around 30 per cent of Chile's GDP is exported and 30 per cent imported,' she explains.

In the financial markets, there is a consensus of opinion about Chile. Banco Santander's Roberto Moreno says, 'Our bank has a strong view of Chile's prospects, not just because of its strong export sector but also its healthy rate of savings (at about 25 per cent of GDP). Its unique pension model has raised national savings, which gives Chile a good source of investment funds and makes it less debt-reliant than its South American neighbours.'

Indeed, Chile has done very well: strong growth, low inflation, a strong export sector and fiscal stability. But Chile wants to ensure that economic success goes hand in hand with democratic and social progress. According to Karen Poniachik, 'We have reduced absolute poverty in Chile and all our social indicators such as education retention rates and literacy have improved remarkably. Chile will continue to invest in human capital to lock in our economic success.'

Many Chile business leaders agree with Poniachik. For instance, Francisco Tomic, Vice-president of Human Resources for Chile's largest company, the government-owned copper producer Codelco, agrees strongly with Poniachik's analysis. Tomic, whose father Radomiro Tomic ran as a centrist Christian Democrat presidential candidate against Salvador

Allende in 1970 and the Right's Jorge Alessandri, believes that good industrial relations are the reason for Chile's economic success as a democratic nation. 'Codelco could not have had the success we have had in growth, employment and exports without the workers and their unions. The union representatives play a key role in devising the company's business plan and the company believes that democratic consultation with the workforce is not only the right thing to do but also makes good business sense,' he explains.

Interestingly, many Chileans are keen to position themselves as a Pacific nation as well as a Latin American one, as Manfred Wilhelmy of the Chile Pacific Foundation comments. 'We admire Australia,' he says, 'we like how they have managed to combine economic progress with social cohesion. It is true that they call us the Latin American jaguar to the Asian tigers, but we want to use our economic success and strategic location to improve the opportunities for our people.'

So what does all this mean for Australia? According to Nigel Warren, Australia's Senior Trade Commissioner in Santiago, Chile is becoming a potential regional hub for Australian companies wanting to do business in Latin America. 'There are fifty Australian businesses here in Santiago and sixty in Chile altogether. Many companies like BHP Billiton have been here for over twenty years, attracted by Chile's mining wealth. But we also have companies like Orica and GHD.' And why have so many Australian companies focused on Chile? According to Warren, 'It is simple. Economic success, social cohesion, political stability and rule of law of course matter. But Chile's investment in infrastructure really helps too.'

Engineering consultancy GHD, headed by Mike Rodd, an easygoing and experienced engineer from Melbourne, has been in Chile since 2003. 'The infrastructure is very good and we've found that it's a good place to base our South American operations,' he says.

Sarah Duncan, Orica's Head of Regional Strategy for South America, agrees. 'I can travel very easily from my base in Santiago to all over the South American continent. Lan [the national carrier, Lan Chile] has great connections and Santiago has excellent facilities. The whole Orica board met in Santiago and were very impressed with Chile,' she says.

Duncan is a rarity—an Australian woman executive in Latin America. She says that despite the Latin macho image, she has found the reality quite different. 'I have very support-ive male colleagues in Orica's South American operations, particularly here in Santiago,' she comments.

So whether it's as presidents or foreign executives, women are doing well in Chile. Perhaps this enhanced role of women in public life is a symbol of modern Chile itself: a mixture of economic success, social progress and demo-cratic stability. This is good news for Chile as it forges ahead as South America's jaguar, a modern, stable and secure economy that acts as a Pacific gateway to the continent.

COMING HOME

22 BRINGING IT ALL HOME TO KATH & KIM

Legendary US politician Tip O'Neill once said, 'All politics is local,' and it's the same with economics. When the airport economist returns home to Australia he gets out and about to the offices, factories and other worksites of our cities and country towns to see where our future export talent lies, and he makes some interesting discoveries. For example, there are strong links between immigration and exports, impressive showings in the bush as well as the city, and a new generation of exporters (dubbed 'Generation eXport'). He also finds a great entrepreneurial culture amongst Australian women— the 'Kath & Kim effect'—who demonstrate that exporting really does make you 'effluent'.

FOR ALL THE travels the airport economist has taken around the world, there's nothing more fascinating than coming home to your own culture with fresh eyes. And when that home is Australia, an economist is particularly lucky as this country has brought in some quite breathtaking economic reforms particularly with the floating of the exchange rate in 1983 by then prime minister Bob Hawke and treasurer Paul Keating. (The market economists in Sydney are actually having a party to celebrate the float's twenty-fifth anniversary—and they say economists have no social life!), The Australian economy has really opened up and businesses, both large and small, in the city or the bush, have embraced some of the opportunities that globalisation has to offer. We may be the lucky country but, thanks to our exporting businesses, we have made our own luck. Floating the dollar, tariff reductions and subsequent reforms in tax, education and training have enabled Australian businesses to gain the confidence to compete globally, and exporters, workers and the Australian community as a whole have benefited.

Exporting is now undertaken by micro (one to four employees) and small (five to nineteen employees) businesses as well as by large companies at the top end of town. According to the Australian Bureau of Statistics, almost 90 per cent of exporters have a turnover of less than $1 million a year, with niche enterprises like Beeline Technologies (GPS software), Bloom Cosmetics and Femme Fatale Cosmetics joining well-known corporates like BHP Billiton, Rio Tinto and Wesfarmers in the export game.

Australian exporters now sell their wares in emerging markets in Asia, Latin America and the Middle East as well as traditional markets in the UK, Europe and North America. Asia is proving to be a big player in this, with fourteen out of twenty of Australia's top exporter destinations being in the Asia-Pacific region. Furthermore, with the growth of China and India, Asia is likely to become an even bigger player for Australian exporters.

Young entrepreneurs—the so-called 'Generation eXport' —are going gangbusters overseas in areas like information technology (IT) software and knowledge-based services, adding to the export earnings brought home by Australia's more experienced players in the 'export heartland' of mining, farming and manufacturing.

Women exporters are also doing well, especially as consumer markets grow in developing countries and women there gain more economic power. Currently women run one-third of Australia's small businesses, and the growth in women-run businesses is accelerating.

Regional Australia is also becoming a great source of global entrepreneurship, building on Australia's traditional rural strengths in mining and agriculture but also grafting IT and services onto primary industry. The bush is also benefiting from a 'sea change' effect, with city professionals setting up in coastal regions for reasons of work and lifestyle balance.

So why has this occurred? After all, exporting has traditionally been a tough game. As all seasoned players know, it takes a lot of hard yakka to venture overseas as prospective businesses have traditionally been hit by a myriad of trade barriers and restrictions. In addition, there are business regulations, red tape and various unofficial delays (known euphemistically as 'non-tariff barriers'). And even if formal trade restrictions were overcome, there were other barriers to contend with such as technological constraints, poor communications and difficulties in transport and logistics. To top it all off, there were cultural and psychological factors that affect business practices overseas.

For many businesses, these impediments together or even in isolation made a successful overseas contract seem like mission impossible, but the times are a-changing when it comes to trade. Fortunately, as a result of trade liberalisation and the associated globalisation of world markets, formal trade barriers are being consistently demolished. This is partly due to multilateral liberalisation under the auspices of the General Agreement on Tariffs and Trade (GATT) and its successor, the World Trade Organization (WTO). The agreements have steadily reduced across-the-board trade barriers since World War II. In addition, in recent years, multilateral liberalisation has been supplemented by regional bilateral deals between key trading partners. In fact, from 1948 to 1994, GATT received 124 regional trade agreements but since the WTO was formed in 1995 there have been 130 agreements notified. Or to put it another way, more bilateral agreements have been notified in the past ten years than in the previous near half century.

All this global trade liberalisation activity is helping us in Australia. Traditionally, Australia has been a leader in trade liberalisation with a strong presence in the WTO and recent success in forging bilateral and regional free trade agreements. And this strategy has been bearing fruit as recent evidence shows that barriers have been coming down for many Australian exporters. In fact, according to the DHL Export Barometer, almost one-third of exporters (32 per cent) surveyed said they faced no barriers at all when venturing offshore. The rest of the barriers were business/cultural barriers (18 per cent), the regulatory environment (17 per cent), strength of competition (17 per cent) and set-up costs (16 per cent). Language barriers constituted 13 per cent whilst formal tariff barriers accounted for only 11 per cent of those surveyed.

However, there are also technological barriers to contend with, though improvements in IT have certainly helped exporters in terms of marketing. For example, the Internet has enabled exporters—from Kings Cross to Kukerin—to sell their wares instantaneously to a global market. A famous example is Mary Nenke's of Cambinata Yabbies in rural Western Australia, who started a website to sell yabbies to Perth but ended up selling to the USA, Singapore, Hong Kong and more as a result of the Internet. And she is not alone. In fact, the increase in small businesses exporting has been associated with the rise of the Internet. According to Sensis, more exporters, large and small, have quickly taken up the World Wide Web than domestic businesses, reducing the marketing constraints associated with our 'tyranny of distance'.

But in this new, open world, Australia has still been able to embrace its own culture—and in some cases export it to the rest of the world. One of Australia's greatest hits in terms of popular culture has been the television series *Kath & Kim*, created by well-known Australian comediennes Jane Turner and Gina Riley. The airport economist's most noted discovery whilst travelling his own backyard is that *Kath & Kim* can help us better understand the importance of exporting for Australia. Not convinced? Well, in the immortal words of Kath, 'look at moie, look at moie, look at moie, look at moie' and I'll tell you why.

First, there's the 'F' factor—Fountain Lakes. Kath and Kim's home suburb is one of many outer metropolitan hubs of local small businesses exporting their heads off. According to 'Industry in the Regions', a seminal study by the Australian Industry Group and the Commonwealth Bank, export intensity (export revenue as a share of total revenue generated by locally based companies) is particularly high in outer suburban areas (like the mythical Fountain Lakes) and in regional Australia.

Second, *Kath & Kim*'s creators, Jane Turner and Gina Riley, are part of a growing number of women entrepreneurs, many of whom are exporting. As already mentioned, women run one-third of Australia's small businesses and there has been a significant increase in the number of businesses operated by women relative to blokes. In fact, one of the fastest growing areas for women entrepreneurs is north-west Melbourne (which, of course, incorporates Moonee Ponds, home of that other famous Australian suburban cultural export, Dame Edna). Valuable global brands like Bloom, Femme Fatale and 3C are all run by women (although Kim's idea for a company, 'Hornbag Exports', may not translate so well in some countries).

Third, there's the importance of aptitude and attitude in exporting. According to Sydney University's Professor of Marketing Chris Styles, many companies have the right aptitude (skills, product, brand) but not attitude (commitment to exporting, building partnerships). Kath has the right aptitude and a positive attitude, whilst Kim's attitude needs a little work (as she says to her daughter, 'Stop whingeing, Epponnee-Rae, it's Mummy's turn now').

Fourth, in exporting, partnerships matter. International business is a bit like a marriage—you've got to be loyal and work it through. An Austrade/University of New South Wales study showed that many Australian businesses survived the Asian financial crisis because they stuck with their Asian business partners when things went pear-shaped and benefited when they improved. Kath and her husband Kel (played by Glenn Robbins) also have a very successful and positive joint venture happening that should survive through thick and through thin.

Fifth, exporting is all about innovation. As a creative type of butcher, Kel is always experimenting with his gourmet sausage. Austrade research shows that like Kel, exporters are innovators, constantly introducing a new brand or product into the market or trying out a new service (that is, something 'noice, unusual, different').

Sixth, we need exports to pay for our imports—that is why we export in the first place. Brett Craig (Kim's long-suffering husband, played by Peter Rowsthorn) works for an electronics outlet that sells many imported IT products and gadgets. Basically, Australia sells lots of products that we are good at producing—cars, wine, wheat, wool, education, mining software, farming technology—so we can import what we consume. In *Kath & Kim* language, we need to export Kel's gourmet sausages so we can import Brett's floppy disks.

Seventh, there are strong connections between trade and sport, and that's where Kim's second best friend, Sharon Strzelecki (Magda Szubanski), comes in. Sharon knows that exporters are like Australia's world-champion cricket and netball teams: they compete with the world's best on a global stage. As a result, they improve their skills, training, productivity and innovation—like Warnie's flipper. They also enable other companies to be exporters—like Albion, the makers of the Australian cricket team's baggy green cap and helmets.

Sharon was aiming (unsuccessfully, as it happened) to be a volunteer at Melbourne's Commonwealth Games in 2006 and knows the importance of special events for exporting. Many exporters got their start at the 2000 Sydney Olympics, picked up contracts for Athens in 2004 and did well in the race for lucrative contracts at Beijing in 2008 and London in 2012. To take advantage of Australia's time in the spotlight, the Australian government started the Business Club Australia (BCA) concept, spearheaded by Austrade at Sydney 2000 and the Rugby World Cups of 2003 and 2007. BCA is a networking club to foster business links at major sporting events, and companies like Woodhead architects (featured in the Singapore chapter) are an example of how 'the power of schmooze' can help. BCA has big things planned for the Beijing Olympics in 2008, and has also been involved in the Rugby World Cup 2007 in France, the FINA swimming championships and the Spring Racing Carnival in Melbourne.

Eighth, there's 'the Kylie effect' to consider too. Australian singing sensation Kylie Minogue went from starring in *Neighbours*, the suburban Melbourne-based soap opera, to take on the UK and then the world (and she of course got a cameo in *Kath & Kim*). Like Kylie, many Australian exporters get their start in London. According to Austrade research, there are around 5000 Australian companies exporting to the UK, well ahead of any other European destination (see chapter 17).

So there you have it, *Kath & Kim* can show Australia how to get on the export bandwagon. As Kim herself puts it: 'Exporting makes you effluent, Mum . . . and I want to be effluent.'

Let's hope there's enough 'effluence' to go around as more Australian businesses take on a global journey of their own.

THE AIRPORT ECONOMIST'S TEN COMMANDMENTS

So you've heard all about our exporting success—but how can you join the winners in the global game? Whilst the airport economist is no expert in theology, here are my Ten Commandments to take into account when contemplating the great leap forward into global markets. But remember: like the biblical ten that Moses took from God high on the mount, they are only a guide and cannot be applied to every company in every circumstance.

FIRST, THOU SHALT export for the right reasons. That is, go into something you know about and are passionate about, not as a get-rich-quick scheme. The successful exporters in this book are all passionate people who know their business and their community. Take Mary Nenke, the yabbie exporter from Kukerin in Western Australia (a town of fifty—with Mary's family making up almost ten of those!). Facing a drought, Mary saw opportunity in her farm's side interest in yabbies and organised the community accordingly. She clearly knew her stuff—her market and her community. She wasn't a merchant banker from Perth or Sydney 'dabbling' in a hobby on the promise that it would make money.

SECOND, if you've got local knowledge, flaunt it! Remember the Vakulin family in Russia? They settled in Port

172

Adelaide after emigrating from the former Soviet Union, and so had the Russian language and a strong network of ready-made local contacts on their side when they set up offices in their former homeland. It's cases like this that show how important immigration has been to Australia. The stories of Jimmy Du in China or Paul Lee and Jim Lim in South Korea also show the possible trade links that can be forged through immigration. In fact, over 50 per cent of our export businesses are run by owners or managers born outside Australia.

THIRD, if you don't have migrant community links, use the expatriate network. If sport is your thing, join the Shanghai Tigers or Beijing Bombers footy clubs in China; if you prefer a professional organisation, Advance or the American Australian Association in New York or Sundowners in Bangkok may be the link you need. The networks you'll make will help your business—and you can have fun at the same time!

FOURTH, thou shalt take advantage of big events. How did a local architecture firm like Woodhead succeed in the Asian market? It leveraged off *the* big event—Sydney's 2000 Olympics—by using Business Club Australia. It's the same for rugby in France, football in South Africa, horseracing in Melbourne or Dubai and the Olympics in Beijing and London. These types of events will be 'critical mass' in terms of clients, customers, investors and potential business partners and, for an up-and-coming exporter, could be the opportunity of a business lifetime.

FIFTH, thou shalt not shy away from celebrity endorsement. How did a small family business in Western Australia like Ganehill crack the Italian market? It used celebrity endorsement from someone Italians can't get enough of, Megan Gale. This certainly worked well in Italy, and it works in other markets too. Remember, for instance, that Australian cricketers Brett Lee and Matthew Hayden were big news in the Indian market. Just getting a celebrity on board gives your product automatic brand recognition, but it will of course work even better if the endorser really understands and likes your product. For example, Megan Gale was very clear in our interview that she endorsed the Ganehills range because it was sun-smart. The other benefit of this strategy is that it gave the airport economist an interview that was a lot of fun to do as well! Let's call that a 'positive' externality.

SIXTH, thou shalt use education networks as much as possible. Remember my old dorm mates? Raymond Lim and his fellow Adelaide University graduates are now bigwigs in Singapore, so joining university alumni associations—especially in places like Singapore, Kuala Lumpur and London—could help you too.

SEVENTH, thou shalt heed market diversity. Many countries are mysteries to us and remain so even after we visit them a lot, so it's important to always take cultural and geographical diversity into account. What goes down well in New York may not work in Kansas City, and the same goes in a large country like China or Russia. So be mindful of regional differences and take advantage of Austrade's vast network, spread far and wide beyond just the capital cities and major financial centres. And watch out for intellectual property issues, even in the USA or other countries where a common language is spoken.

EIGHTH, thou shalt seek assistance when needed. As well as taking advantage of Austrade's global network, the Export Finance and Insurance Corporation can help you assess country risk, Austrade's corporate partners can assist with legal and accounting issues, banks can give exchange rate risk and export finance information, and the various state government and industry associations have export advice and training programmes. And use the government network of your partner country too and avoid being duped by the 'friend of a friend' or so-called cousin of the person you sat next to on the plane over—there are plenty of dodgy middle-men in all markets and you don't want to risk flying blind. Also remember that despite the eventual rewards, getting into exporting is expensive so don't forget to check out the Export Market Development Grants scheme (EMDG) for help in reducing the cost of marketing when establishing yourself overseas.

NINTH, thou shalt remember that relationships matter. As the chapter on Argentina shows, it takes two to tango. So work on your relationships and stick with your business partners through thick and through thin. Many Australian exporters survived the Asian crisis because they proved they were loyal business partners, not carpetbaggers who got going as soon as things got tough. The same goes for the workplace. On average, exporters pay higher wages than non-exporters and are better bosses in terms of job security, employment conditions, training and career development. This really matters because when you are running an export business, with all the time zones, travel and trade diplomacy that is involved, you need a bunch of 'goers' in your team who know their loyalty is highly valued.

TENTH, remember that you are not alone! There are over 44,000 Aussie exporters thriving in the global market. And many of them had a rough start, but got help when they needed it and are now great Australian exporters. So now go forth and export!

THE AIRPORT ECONOMIST'S USEFUL WEBSITES IN TRADE AND ECONOMICS

For Australians doing business overseas, students and anyone with an interest in what makes the global economy tick, try the following:

Australian

Australian Bureau of Statistics—www.abs.gov.au

Great for all sorts of data on the Australian economy and society.

Department of Foreign Affairs and Trade—www.dfat.gov.au

DFAT has useful travel information for Australians venturing overseas with embassy addresses, information regarding passport and visa requirements, travel alerts etc.

I also recommend looking at its statistics website, www.dfat.gov.au/publications/statistics_international.html

Australian Business Economists—www.abe.org.au

The ABE is Australia's leading organisation of market economists. It organises great events with guest speakers such as Reserve Bank of Australia governors, Federal treasurers and other leading lights.

Reserve Bank of Australia—www.rba.gov.au

This is a source of great data, speeches and research papers. The bank's chart pack of economic graphs produced by the RBA's economists is first class and well worth looking at.

University of South Australia (internet resources for economists)—www.library.unisa.edu.au/resources/subject/econo mic.asp

This site is great for economics teachers and students.

Australian Trade Commission (Austrade)—www.austrade. gov.au and Export Finance and Insurance Corporation (EFIC)—www.efic.gov.au

For practical export information, exporters and potential exporters should look at both these sites.

Smart Company—www.smartcompany.com.au

Practical tips for small business.

International

Asian Development Bank—www.adb.org

A good source of research on the Asia Pacific region.

Family Tree of Economists—www-personal.umich.edu/ ~alandear/tree/INDEX.HTM

For the who's who of academic economists in international trade.

Global Trade Negotiations (Harvard University)— www.cid.harvard.edu/cidtrade

A great website initiated by Harvard Development Economist Dani Rodrik which focuses on trade and development issues.

Institute for International Economics—www.iie.com

From Fred Bergsten's prestigious international trade think tank in Washington DC.

International Labour Organisation—www.ilo.org

For international labour market issues.

International Monetary Fund—www.imf.org

The Fund produces its World Economic Outlook and other major research papers on this site. The IMF Data Mapper is very useful for number crunchers looking for comparative data.

Organisation for Economic Co-operation and Development—www.oecd.org

An excellent site from the well-respected Paris think tank. The *OECD Observer* is worth looking at for a synthesis of topical international economic issues.

Research papers in economics—www.repec.org

If you want to find anything that's ever been written in academic economics you'll find it here.

United Nations Conference on Trade and Development—www.unctad.org/trade

This UN body publishes some good papers and data bases, particularly on foreign investment.

World Bank—www.worldbank.org

The World Bank has a great many resources online about economic development. The Bank's Development Gateways are worth looking at, particularly the one on trade policy issues at: www.developmentgateway.org/trade/

World Trade Organization—www.wto.org

The WTO's annual *World Trade Report* (which can be down-loaded online) tells you everything you need to know about trade in the world in any given year. You can also look up trade data on this site. It's pretty comprehensive.

Blogs

There are also a number of columnists and blogs the airport economist enjoys including:

Martin Wolf in the *Financial Times*—www.ft.com/comment/columnists/martinwolf

Paul Krugman in the *New York Times*—www.topics.nytimes.com/top/opinion/editorialsandoped/oped/columnists/paulkrugman

Steve D. Levitt and Stephen J. Dubner, authors of the best-seller *Freakonomics*—www.freakonomics.blogs.nytimes.com

Tim Harford, author of *The Undercover Economist*—www.timharford.com

Philippe Le Grain, author of *Open World*—www.philippelegrain.com

The *New Economist* blog site—www.neweconomist.blogs.com

Andrew Leigh with new ideas on economics, politics and current events from an Antipodean perspective—www.andrewleigh.com

John Quiggin—www.johnquiggin.com

Nick Gruen—www.gruen.com.au

Alan   Mitchell   in   the   *Australian   Financial   Review*—
www.afr.com

Ross Gittins in the *Sydney Morning Herald* and *The Age*—
www.smh.com.au/news/opinion/rossgittins   and   www.
theage.com.au/news/opinion/RossGittins

Business Review Weekly—www.brw.com.au

The Australian— www.theaustralian.news.com.au

And wait, there's more . . . the airport economist's own website 'Economists Corner'—www.austrade.gov.au/economists
corner, which links to www.theairporteconomist.com

This page includes articles, data, books and other
resources in the wonderful world of trade and economics.
For specific country information check out the Export Snap-
shots, which provide postcards on the country of your choice.

THE A TO Z OF EXPORTING

A is for APEC

Formed by Australia and the Republic of Korea in 1989, Asia Pacific Economic Co-operation, or APEC, is the premier forum for facilitating economic growth, cooperation, trade and investment in the Asia-Pacific region. APEC's 21 members cooperate on areas as diverse as international trade and investment, global security and environmental standards.

APEC is the only inter-governmental group in the world operating on the basis of non-binding commitments, open dialogue and equal respect for the views of all participants. Unlike the World Trade Organization or other multilateral trade bodies, APEC has no treaty obligations required of its participants. Decisions made within APEC are reached by consensus and commitments are undertaken on a voluntary basis. APEC's twenty-one members—referred to as 'Member Economies'—account for approximately 41 per cent of the world's population, approximately 56 per cent of world GDP and about 49 per cent of world trade.

Member economies are: Australia, Brunei Darussalam, Canada, Chile, People's Republic of China, Hong Kong China, Indonesia, Japan, Republic of Korea, Malaysia, Mexico, New Zealand, Papua New Guinea, Peru, the Republic of the Philippines, the Russian Federation, Singapore, Chinese Taipei, Thailand, United States of America, Vietnam.

www.apec.org

B is for Business Club Australia

Business Club Australia is a free membership-based business matching program that helps to create international business opportunities against the backdrop of major sporting events. To date, successful programs have been designed and implemented for the Sydney 2000 Olympics, Rugby World Cup 2003, Melbourne 2006 Commonwealth Games, the 2006 Melbourne Cup Carnival, the 12th FINA World Swimming Championships and the 2008 Beijing Olympic Games. BCA has held over 260 networking events in Australia and overseas. There are around 8500 members—with some 37 per cent located offshore—and the BCA program has facilitated over $1.7 billion in trade and investment deals since 2000. That certainly shows the economics of networking—or 'the power of schmooze'—works in practice.

www.businessclubaustralia.com.au

C is for China

What more can be said of China? The Middle Kingdom is one of modern history's major economic success stories and a booming export market for Australia. Australia sells coal, iron ore, aluminium and LNG by the boatload to Beijing, but we are also seeing great success in professional services, education, tourism and agribusiness as well. And many Australian businesses are 'hugging the Panda' now. According to Austrade research, there are over 4200 Australian companies exporting to China in goods alone, illustrating that you don't just have to be BHP Billiton, Woodside or Rio Tinto to be successful there. To help exporters navigate this amazing country, Austrade has thirteen points of contact in

China (with major offices in Beijing, Shanghai, and Guangzhou). In addition, Austrade has offices in Hong Kong and Taipei and representation in Macau and Kaohsiung.

D is for Dubai and the United Arab Emirates

Dubai in the United Arab Emirates (UAE) is a boom town for Australian exporters looking to do business in the Middle East. The self-styled 'Singapore of the Middle East', Dubai is an *entrepot* (or trading hub) and a major centre for finance, transport and logistics for the Gulf region. There are thought to be over 15,000 Australian expatriates in the UAE in the banking, finance, architectural services, construction, retail, education and health sectors. In fact, Dubai is so Australian now that the AFL hosted a pre-season NAB Cup game there between the Adelaide Crows and the Collingwood Magpies.

E is for E-M-D-G

Every budding exporter should see if they are eligible for an Export Market Development Grant (EMDG). This is a key Australian Government financial assistance programme for aspiring and current exporters. Administered by Austrade, the scheme supports a wide range of industry sectors and products, including inbound tourism and the export of intellectual property and know-how outside Australia.

The EMDG scheme:

- encourages small and medium-sized Australian businesses to develop export markets;
- reimburses up to 50 per cent of expenses incurred on eligible export promotion activities, above a $15,000 threshold;
- provides up to seven grants to each eligible applicant.

To access the scheme for the first time, businesses need to have spent $15,000 over two years on eligible export marketing expenses.

www.austrade.gov.au/What-Is-EMDG

F is for franchising

Many Australian exporters adopt a franchise model when setting up businesses in a new country under their brand. Australian companies such as Boost Juice, Gloria Jeans, Cookie Man and Baker's Delight are all doing well in markets from Mumbai to Mexico. Of course, Australia's most famous franchise exporter is the children's entertainment group The Wiggles, who were also Australia's Exporter of the Year in 2005. There are now Mandarin and Spanish language versions of The Wiggles making children laugh, dance and sing in Asia and Latin America. According to Cheryl Scott, Austrade's franchising guru: 'It's really important to get good business partners/master franchisees, as you have to protect your brand carefully. You can be pro-active about this through careful selection in the first instance, but also thorough ongoing training and development so everyone feels part of the team.'

G is for GATT

The General Agreement on Tariffs and Trade (GATT) was set up at the Bretton Woods talks in the aftermath of the Second World War. The main aim was to avoid the mistakes of the period after the First World War, when protectionist pressures helped exacerbate the Great Depression. The GATT 'Rounds' encouraged countries to negotiate the reduction of protectionist tariffs and subsidies multilaterally to help enhance economic development. The final GATT Round, which became known as the 'Uruguay Round', was completed in 1994. (See U is for Uruguay Round.)

H is for hedging

In a world of fluctuating exchange rates, some exporters choose to undertake 'hedging' in their contacts to mitigate against changes in the exchange rate. That is, they may agree at a fixed exchange rate or a fixed price into the future, or they may take out insurance against exchange rate risk. Some exporters also carry accounts in US dollars or Japanese yen as a 'natural hedge'. According to research by Austrade and DHL, around 24 per cent of large and 25 per cent of medium-sized exporters engage in some form of hedging (compared to only 5 per cent of small exporters and 4 per cent of micros). So even if you're a small or medium-sized exporter, hedging is clearly an option.

Paul Edwards, Senior Manager Risk Management Advisory for HSBC, advises that exporters should always look to hedge. 'Hedging is an insurance against the swings and roundabouts that are commonplace in foreign exchange markets. Hedging allows you to lock in profits. It's important for exporters to remember they are not in the business of running foreign exchange positions but rather selling "widgets". By covering foreign exchange exposures, exporters will be able to focus on their underlying business rather than being exposed to the fluctuations and vagaries of global financial markets.' Ian Rogers of HSBC's Cardiff headquarters recommends that exporters set up a foreign exchange account in US dollars as it 'provides a natural hedge ... I would also look into insurance, products from EFIC [Export Finance Insurance Corporation] like Headway and other risk mitigants beyond the traditional letter of credit,' he suggests.

So, in short, hedging is an option and there are many financial services available to prospective exporters who will have to deal with a dancing dollar in world markets.

I is for India

There's no doubt that after a slow start, India has become a real pin-up for economic reform. Since India's Prime Minister Dr Manmahon Singh started the reform process when he was finance minister in the early 1990s, the sub-continent has gone from strength to strength, breaking the shackles of its 'Licence Raj' days to be a major hub for IT and professional services. The Australian–Indian trade relationship is now becoming more than 'the 3 "c"s' of cricket, curry and Commonwealth with nearly 2000 Australian businesses now exporting goods to India. As a result, Austrade has expanded its Indian network with locations in Chandigarh, Chennai, Hyderabad, Kolkata, Mumbai and New Delhi as well as representation in Pakistan, Bangladesh and Sri Lanka.

J is for joint venture

In some markets it makes sense to get together with a local partner to form a joint venture or a strategic alliance rather than setting up by yourself. According to research by Austrade and Sensis, exporting and importing are still the most important activities in internationalisation (accounting for 67 per cent of all small and medium-sized enterprises that go global), but around 9 per cent of enterprises were engaged in joint ventures with a foreign partner. The rest were involved in franchising, licensing, foreign direct investment and foreign aid procurement. Talk to Austrade before you set up a joint venture as there can be important legal procedures to be aware of in foreign markets, and it is important to choose the right partner so your business life doesn't end up like a Hollywood marriage.

K is for Kununurra

Kununurra is a thriving town in the north-west of Australia and, like many rural and regional centres, Austrade is there to help its local businesses go global. With its eighteen national offices and fifty-one Tradestart offices (including eight Export Hubs), Austrade has regional Australia covered back home as well as around the globe.

L is for licensing

In some markets, exporters can consider licensing. That is, you allow a local company to produce your product whilst receiving a royalty or licensing fee for your intellectual property. Manufacturing exporters often do this if set-up costs in a country are too prohibitive. In some countries you also need export licences, so check this out with Austrade well before you set up.

M is for managing

In general, Austrade research shows that exporters make good managers. On average, exporters pay 60 per cent higher wages than non-exporters and they also invest more in education and training and occupational health and safety, and provide better job security. So part of being a good exporter is being a good employer. Exporters also are more likely to promote women as CEOs or as their head of exporting, so watch out for some great Aussie female entre-preneurial talent hitting trade shows and airport lounges in years to come!

N is for N-E-D-P

According to Austrade and the Australian Bureau of Statistics there are over 44,000 exporters in Australia, but they didn't arrive out of thin air. For many, it took a lot of preparation. Accordingly, Austrade set up the New Exporter Development Programme (NEDP) to help the rookies get some training through export coaching and workshops on pricing, risk management, freight and logistics.

O is for opportunity

Opportunity is what exporting is all about. Austrade research shows that 50 per cent of all exporters are 'accidental'; that is, they didn't intend to go global but an opportunity fell their way. Austrade's international network is bursting with opportunities and its job is to find Australian companies ready to stand and deliver.

P is for planning

While many exporters say they got into the global game by accident or by chance, once they're in it pays to plan. The majority of successful exporters have an export plan that enables them to expand their business and ensure that they develop the capacity to meet future demand. Austrade deals with thousands of export plans and can help new exporters with their own plan when starting out.

Q is for Qantas

Qantas—the flying kangaroo—began as a small carrier servicing the Australian outback from its rural headquarters in Longreach. It's now one of the world's oldest and safest international airlines and has been serving Australian exporters since its early years. Qantas is also a major export earner in its own right as it carries thousands of international tourists, students and business travellers daily to and from Australia. One of Qantas' 747s (named 'Wunala dreaming') was famously painted by Balarinji, an indigenous Australian design company started by John and Ros Moriarty.

R is for risk

With the volatility of global markets and geo-political events, exporting is not a risk-free business, especially for small- and medium-sized enterprises (SMEs). Fortunately, exporters have many supportive government services at their disposal. The Department of Foreign Affairs and Trade can help with passports, travel warnings and consular assistance, Austrade can reduce the cost and risk of doing business offshore, and the

Export Finance Insurance Corporation (EFIC) can provide insurance and other financial products to help minimise risk. As an export credit agency, EFIC operates beyond the limits of the commercial market. It provides the support exporters need when financial, country or industry risks exceed the capacity available in financial markets. *EFIC Headway* is particularly focused on the risk assessment needs of SMEs.

www.efic.gov.au

S is for services

While Australia is a major exporter of commodities in mining and agribusiness—the so-called 'rocks and crops' end of the exporter community—services matter too. Services are 'everything that you can't drop on your foot', from ballet dancers to lawyers, architects to hairdressers, teachers to technicians. Many services are also related to mining and agriculture; that's why you'll meet Western Australian software trainers in Siberia and South Australian viticulture marketers in South America. Austrade has specialists dedicated to the services industries in areas such as finance, sports marketing and arts and entertainment, all likely to be big players in Australia's export future.

T is for Tradestart

Tradestart is a network of Austrade offices and associated points of contact in Australia designed to help potential exporters get a footing in the international marketplace. Tradestart is a partnership between Austrade, state and territory governments, industry associations and regional development organisations, all of whom have access to the Austrade network and services. There are over fifty Tradestart offices in rural and regional Australia from the Top End to Tasmania. (See also K is for Kununurra.)

U is for Uruguay Round

The Uruguay Round was the last of the GATT rounds of multilateral negotiations. The negotiations began in Punta del Este, Uruguay, in 1986 (hence the name Uruguay Round) and were completed in Marrakesh, Morocco, in 1994. To help agricultural nations better negotiate in the Uruguay Round, Australia established the 'Cairns Group' of agricultural exporters in 1986 to fight trade distorting agricultural subsidies and other forms of protectionism.

V is for Vietnam

The latest Asian Tiger to emerge, Vietnam has overcome war and disruption to become one of the fastest growing economies in Southeast Asia. Vietnam's willingness to open its economy has delivered results. Its economic growth rate has averaged 7.5 per cent annually—second only to China in the Asia-Pacific region. The reform process—known as *Doi Moi* or 'renewal'—has delivered improvements in Vietnamese living standards and sharp reductions in poverty. As a result, Vietnam has become a real poster boy for economic development. The World Bank estimates that today around 30 per cent of Vietnam's population live below the poverty line compared to 60 per cent in the early 1990s. Australian exporters are active in Vietnam in telecommunications, education, steel, engineering, tourism and in the financial services sector.

W is for the World Trade Organization

The World Trade Organization (WTO) is the successor to the GATT and was established in 1995 following the completion of the Uruguay Round. The WTO is responsible for facilitating multilateral negotiations between its member countries, setting a rules framework for engagement in international trade (including dispute settlement) and for helping facilitate the negotiation of regional trade agreements. The WTO has welcomed many developing countries—such as China

and Vietnam—into its fold since its inception but has found
the negotiation of the Doha Development Round (the
successor to the Uruguay Round) slow going due to stum-
bling blocks such as agriculture and the proliferation of
bilateral trade agreements between member states.

X is for Xian

X is for Xian, home of the famous Terracotta Warriors and
one of Austrade's thirteen points of contact in the People's
Republic of China. (See C is for China.)

Y is for yen

Yen is the currency of Australia's longstanding trading
partner, Japan. While most Australian exporters are paid in
either Australian dollars or US dollars (greenbacks), some
choose to be paid in yen or euros (the European Union's
currency) or hold an account in yen (see H is for hedging).
Japan attracts around nearly 3600 Australian exporters each
year, although only around 100 Australian businesses have
permanent offices in Japan.

Z is for Zagreb

Zagreb is where Austrade has its headquarters for Croatia.
Since the end of the Cold War, Central, Southern and
Eastern Europe have started to rebuild their economies
and Australian exporters are returning to these markets—
particularly those that have recently joined the European
Union. Croatia, which also had to withstand the wars following the break-up of the former Yugoslavia, has attracted some
Australian exporters in food, wine, agribusiness, infrastructure and education.

ACKNOWLEDGEMENTS

First, a big thank you to Patrick Gallagher, executive chairman of Allen & Unwin, Rebecca Kaiser, Editorial Director, and their colleagues Clare Drysdale, Sarah Hickie and Kathy Mossop for taking on *The Airport Economist*. It's a great honour to be with such an icon in Australian publishing and a great Australian exporter in their own right.

Second, thank you to Australia's true 'guru' of economic journalism, Ross Gittins, of the *Sydney Morning Herald* and the *Age*, for his encouragement and guidance in the mysterious craft of economics writing.

Third, thanks to James Lotherington, Gregory Harvey, Dharsh Khandiah, Hala Shash, Kate Pembroke and Tim Sinclair of Austrade for their enthusiasm and encouragement of *The Airport Economist*.

Fourth, to the many people who helped me along the way with travel logistics, story ideas and so on—many thanks. I have tried to remember you all but be sure to let me know if I haven't: Nixon Apple, Alicia Barry, David Bassanese, Frank Bingham, Jose Blanco, John Buchanan, Adam Blight, Fred Brenchley, Nic Brown, Anthony Bubalo, Bill Brummit, The late Tom Burns, Rowan Callick, Stefania Castaldi, Andrew Charlton, Chia Tai Tee, Kevin Chinnery, Florence Chong,

Nick Cohen, Tim Cohen, Tim Colebatch, Jonathan Coppel, Nicholas Coppel, Michael Crawford, David Crook, Blanche d'Alpuget, Karla Davies, Guy Debelle, Leigh Derigo, Ric Deverell, Tim Devinney, Tim Dixon, Roger Donnelly, Leith Doody, Lloyd Downey, Jimmy Du, Jacqui Dwyer, Malcolm Edey, John Edwards, Saul Eslake, Pat Evans, Tony Featherstone, Allan Fels, Mark Fenton-Jones, June Field, Tim Fischer, Steve Fosbery, Richard Freeman, Michael Fullilove, Megan Gale, Purnima Ganapathy, John Garnaut, Ross Garnaut, David Garner, Tim Gauci, Kieran Gilbert, Dennis Godfrey, Amanada Gome, Josh Gordon, Jenny Graham, Sid Gray, Roy Green, Bob Gregory, Stephen Grenville, Michael Growder, David Gruen, Nick Gruen, Allan Gyngell, Joan Hardkte, Brett Henderson, Kym Hewett, Gosia Hill, Kevin Hopgood-Brown, Barry Hughes, Peter Ironmonger, Jessica Irvine, David James, Maureen Jordan, Simon Kelly, Sarkis Khoury, Cleve Killiby, Jo Kim, Phua Kok Kim, David Koch, James Kondo, Glenda Korporaal, Miles Kupa, Duyet Le Van, Paul Lee, Martine Letts, Corinne Lim, Janice Lim, Jim Lim, Raymond Lim, Tanya Lim, Terrie Lloyd, Stephen Long, Damien Lynch, Cameron MacMillan, Sid Marris, Ikuko Matsumoto, Samantha Mattila, Ross McGregor, The late Morgan Mellish, Kylie Merritt, Rod Morehouse, Alan Morrell, Les Murray, James Myers, Peter O'Byrne, The late Liz O'Neill, Peter Ong, Tracy Ong, Peter Osborne, Bill Pheasant, Ben Potter, Geoff Raby, Betina Reid, J.David Richardson, Peter Roberts, Di Robinson, Dani Rodrik, Michael Roux, Colleen Ryan, Bernard Salt, Robert Samuel, Jacob Saulwick, Stephen Schwartz, Hala Shash, Stephen Shepherd, Michael Short, Christena Singh, Insheok Shim, Fiona Smith, Ian Smith, Laurie Smith, Min-Joo Sohn, Glenn Stevens, Patrick Stringer, Michael Stutchbury, Chris Styles, Penny Styles, Tracey Sutherland, Peter Switzer, Kim Song Tan, Mark Thirlwell, Geoff Tooth, Jeff Turner, David Twine, David Varga, Matt Wade, Michelle Wade, Michael Wadley, Martin Walsh (Austrade), Martin Walsh (Megan Gale's

Australian manager), Bernard Wheelahan, Martin Wolf, Ian Wing, Christopher Wright, John Zubrzycki.

Finally, and most importantly, thanks to my wife, Jo, and daughter, Yun Shi, for putting up with 'Baba's' frequent absences from home whilst I was playing airport economist— and for putting up with my frequent absences *at* home, too!